What do you do when you are desperately wishing for a job promotion and you pray for prosperity but you lose your job instead?

What do you do when you ask God to heal you but you get worse?

What do you do when you agonize in prayer over a loved one in trouble and the loved one is not delivered?

What do you do?

In *Yet Will I Trust Him,* by Peg Rankin, you'll discover what it *really* means to trust God....

Yet Will I Trust Him

Peg Rankin

GL Regal Books A Division of G/L Publications
Glendale, California, U.S.A.

Other good Regal reading:
Autobiography of God by Lloyd John Ogilvie
When There Is No Miracle by Robert L. Wise
How to Cope by Lloyd H. Ahlem

The foreign language publishing of all Regal books is under the direction of GLINT. GLINT provides financial and technical help for the adaptation, translation and publishing of books in more than 85 languages for millions of people worldwide.

For more information write: GLINT, P.O. Box 6688, Ventura, CA 93003.

Scripture quotations in this publication are from the Authorized King James Version of the Bible.

Published by Regal Books Division, G/L Publications
Glendale, California 91209
Printed in U.S.A.

Library of Congress Catalog Card No. 79-91705
ISBN 0-8307-0741-7

Cover photo by Herbert Petermann

This book is lovingly dedicated
to my husband Lee,
whose thoughts are so entwined
with mine that it is impossible
to separate them.

A special thanks
to Mary Sue for typing,
to Judy for proofreading,
and to Lee for enduring.

Contents

Introduction

Just as I was stuffing in my last bite of cherry pie, the phone rang. I thought to myself, "The day has already been full enough. Now what?"

I knew by the pitch of the voice that the call was urgent. "Would you come over right away?" she asked. "We're having a family crisis."

That was all. No hint as to the nature of the problem. I didn't probe.

My husband Lee and I dropped our boys off at the church for a youth activity, then turned our car in the direction of the crisis. We had been called by a friend to help in time of need. That was all we knew. Our mutual silence in the car showed our feelings of inadequacy. I was hoping that Lee would be able to help. He told me later that he was relying on *me*.

In minutes we pulled up in front of a stately colonial. The manicured lawn belied the turmoil that lay within the home. As Lee turned off the ignition, he looked at me and said, "I have no idea what we'll be encountering in there, but let's stop a moment for prayer.

"Dear God," he prayed, "we need your grace and compassion. Let it show to these dear folks inside this home. Give us wisdom to point out sin, if sin is involved. And give us love to heal the wound that sin has caused. In Christ's name. Amen.''

We were met by the father of the family. Mechanically, we exchanged niceties. As he escorted us into the living room, we felt as if we were wading through tension. The mother smiled politely, then began, ''Our daughter moved out tonight. She says we're too strict in our discipline.''

Being a rather strict disciplinarian himself, my husband asked, ''What kind of rules does she want?''

''She wants to choose the company she keeps, to give no account of her whereabouts, and to stay out all night if she wants to. I can't understand it. We aren't perfect parents by any means, but we have tried to show her love. She seems to resent our faith. It's a threat to her independence, I guess. We've made lots of mistakes in trying to share it with her, I admit, and I wish we could do it over. But everybody makes mistakes, don't they? And their kids don't pack up and leave home.''

''Everybody does make mistakes,'' Lee assured her. ''It's what we do with those mistakes that counts. Where is she going to live?''

The mother's eyes filled with tears. ''With her boyfriend,'' she choked. ''He said she could come stay with him.''

In the stillness of that hurting home, we prayed with the mother and father. As Lee brought their petitions before a God who cares, his voice broke with the weight of his compassion. For deep inside he knew that this severance of family relationships could have happened in our home instead of in our friends'! In fact, it could happen in anybody's home. For children have a way of leaping over love, discipline, and reputation. And they don't seem to care whom they hurt.

After talking the situation over and trying to be as helpful as possible, we embraced the parents and left, freshly aware that crises are part of life. What we didn't know at that moment was that this particular crisis was the first in a series of events that would send us to God for greater insight.

It wasn't long after this enounter that Shirley appeared on my doorstep. Shirley is an attractive woman. But lately I noticed a drawn look around her face. Casually, I attributed the look to a crash diet that had squeezed Shirley's figure from a size 14 down to a size 6. The determination and perseverance with which she had attacked her weight problem intrigued me.

This particular morning, though, Shirley looked especially haggard. As she passed through the extended storm door, I thought I smelled alcohol on her breath. She refused an invitation to sit down and share coffee. For what seemed like an eternity, she fidgeted with her car keys, looking at the rug. Finally she blurted out, "We're getting divorced." She fought her tears, then lost.

A wave of compassion swept over me. It is a widely publicized fact that almost half the marriages entered into today end in divorce. But it is one thing to know statistics and quite another thing to know a friend who has suddenly become part of those statistics.

I had suspected that Shirley's marriage was not a happy one. A particularly difficult child was straining the relationship. But I knew that the marriage could be saved if the partners wanted it to be. Obviously, they didn't.

Shirley informed me, "He's leaving me for another woman. I've tried everything, but his mind is made up. He wants to start over."

Wanting to help, I promised Shirley that I would pray for her. She reminded me that such statements upset her. So I quietly listened as she continued her story.

"I feel like a common criminal," she said. "They're going to serve me with papers tomorrow. I can't live like this. I wake up at 2:00 in the morning, reaching for comfort; but comfort is never there."

I wanted to introduce Shirley to life's great Comforter, but she wasn't ready to meet Him. Until she came to that point in her life where she was willing to cast her crisis upon Him, there would be no emotional healing. She would continue to hurt. And I would continue to feel bad for her.

As I bade her good-bye, I touched her hand. Her eyes filled with tears. Somebody cared. Her glance was brief but meaningful. It told me that she knew where she could turn for help when she was willing. But she was not yet willing. Quickly she dropped her eyes.

When they returned to meet mine, they were cold. I could see that her own special method for dealing with crises had taken over. It was a method that I had been watching her perfect ever since our first meeting. She would act nonchalant, convincing herself that everything would turn out all right whether in fact it would or not. In front of others her life would be a pretense.

She sped out of the driveway with a recklessness that concerned me. As I stood in the doorway waving, I wondered how God would use her crisis. Would He draw her to Himself, freeing her will to serve Him? Or would He continue to let her go her own way? If this crisis were not the spiritual turning point in her life, what would be? My speculation disturbed me.

As I walked back into the kitchen, I answered the jangling phone. It was a friend. "Did you hear about Bob?" she queried.

"No, what?" I asked.

I had seen Bob in the hall at the church on Sunday. We had chatted awhile about a mutual friend who was giving up a lucrative job to become a missionary.

"That's what I'd like to do someday," Bob had said, "become a missionary. I guess one of these days I'll just have to take the bull by the horns and do it. I'm not getting any younger, you know. Just turned 40 last week."

With the conversation only a couple of days old, I expected my friend to announce that Bob had come to a decision to give his life to Christ in a full-time missionary effort.

But it was not to be. The voice on the phone shattered my thoughts. "Bob was struck by a car and killed on his way to work this morning," it said, hesitating between the phrases. "His wife is stunned. And the kids—they're so young to be without a daddy. What will they do?"

"They will have to cope with the crisis," I philosophized, startling myself with the starkness of what I was saying, "and go on from there. What else is there to do?"

As I hung up the phone, I had the same helpless feeling that I had experienced when dealing with the family whose rebellious daughter had just run away from home. Then I thought of Shirley and her divorce. Problems seemed to be multiplying everywhere.

Someone has said, "When your world is badly shaken, start with what you know you believe and build upward from there." I decided to put the advice into practice.

I thought, "I know that God is in control of all things. I believe that His plan for our lives is perfect. At least that is what the Bible says. But how can I toss such a platitude to someone caught in the maelstrom of a crisis? Especially when I'm not even sure that I have hold of it myself?"

I was confronted with what I felt has to be accomplished in my own life and in the lives of many others. Somehow we Christians have to get the sovereignty of God out of the Scriptures and into the mainstream of living. But how do we go about doing it? Victory on the mountain peaks is easy. It is a natural result of success. But if Christianity doesn't work in the valleys, it isn't worth having at all, is it?

A week passed. Lee and I were asked to team-teach an elective course for adults in our church's Daily Vacation Bible School. The topic suggested was, "The Sovereignty of God in Family Crises."

The timing of this request overwhelmed us. Had God been preparing us for such a study? The more we thought about it, the more convinced we became that He had been. Therefore, we accepted the challenge. We wanted answers for ourselves. And certainly we wanted them for our friends. But how should we go about preparing for such an awesome responsibility?

The first thing we decided to do was to write down some crises that we had faced in our own lives. Our list turned out heavier than we had expected it to be, for we had not considered our life together to be especially hard. Nevertheless, our scribbles included the following: severe problems with in-laws, the birth of unexpected twins, the early death of Peg's father, the failure of our business, and the placing of Lee's mother in a nursing home. Even though the list was only partial, each event we wrote down evoked vividly painful memories. We remembered how consumed we were by every crisis. In fact, at the time each event was occurring, there was hardly a moment to think of simply living.

The next thing we did was to list crises that different friends of ours had faced—crises that personally we had been spared. There was the long, agonizing death of a spouse, the fatal accident of a teenager, the debilitating illness of a mother, severe financial reversals, marital separation ending in divorce, rebellion in a child, and the carefully planned suicide of a loved one. On and on the list went.

Then we thought about small, daily crises—those problems from which nobody is immune. There is tension between personalities, overloaded schedules at work, inadequate time to accomplish everything that has to be done in a day, and constant disappointments and frustrations.

My husband Lee got so burdened by the impact of this exercise that he blurted, "Good grief! All life is a crisis. It's a crisis to be born. A crisis to die. And a crisis every step in between." At that point I felt like agreeing with him.

To boost our spirits, we reminded ourselves that we had been teaching the Bible for 18 years—we should know what God has to say about crises. As we began preparing this course on family crises, however, we were wishing that our experience in the Word of God were twice that number of years. Then our teaching would be filtered through the wisdom of age. But it wasn't, so we determined to contribute what we could. We decided to teach what we knew to be truth and to discipline ourselves to keep quiet in areas where we had not yet received answers.

Because there would be many different types of crises represented in the lives of our class members, we knew that we could not possibly deal with each one in the amount of time allotted to us. So we decided to present truth pertaining to all crises in general. Then the students could specifically apply the teaching to their individual situations. It was up to the Holy Spirit of God to take the teaching from His Word and to combine it with the lives of each of His children in such a way that victory ensued.

With anticipation, we tossed out the questions that would be covered during the course of study:

1. Who is this God I'm trying to serve?
2. Where is He when I need Him most?
3. Why are there crises in my life?
4. What do life's crises accomplish?
5. How can I have victory in the midst of crises?

We know that teachers cannot integrate truth without spending hours in disciplined study. So before we laid our heads on our pillows that night, we pledged ourselves to God afresh to be diligent in our searching of His Word. Then we reaffirmed our faith in a God who controls all things, working them to His glory and to His children's good. As we prayed together, I felt my husband's hand touch mine. Living for Christ is an adventure shared.

Then we rested knowing that we had entrusted our questions to God. I could not help wondering, though, how many answers He would keep to Himself and not share with us at all, at least not while we lived here on earth. I also wondered if He would ever again let us hold questions to our breasts, unuttered. I was beginning to see that questions in motion are the essence of life. Even answers received have to be tossed up again as questions. For each time an answer returns, it spins toward us with a different facet of its truth showing. Exciting, I thought. I could hardly wait for the course to unfold.

What follows are some of the truths we gleaned as we taught that course on family crises. Now we would like to share with you what we have learned with you.

Peg Rankin

PART I

WHO IS GOD?

1. The God of Scripture

Who is this God I'm trying to serve? He is the God of the Scriptures, not a God of our imagination. The men of God who recorded the Scriptures knew Him in many ways: Isaiah called Him *Father* (see 64:8), as did Jesus (see Matt. 6:9); Hebrews says He is our *Helper* (see 13:6); Genesis describes Him as *Judge* (see 18:25); David and Paul both called Him *King* (see Ps. 24:10; 1 Tim. 1:17): David also called Him his *Shepherd* (see Ps. 23:1).

If we are to worship Him in His fullness, we have to accept Him exactly as He describes Himself in His Word, and not create a God as we would like Him to be. We must accept the Scriptures we have difficulty with as well as the ones that are palatable to us. How do we see God today?

One popular concept of God in our modern world is to see Him only as a *God of love*. God is a God of love, but love is only one facet of His many-faceted character. To worship this one aspect of God alone is to create a lopsided God—love at the expense of holiness. God indeed loves, but He loves righteousness. God also hates. He hates sin. And He can love sinful mankind only through Christ, "For God so loved the world, that he gave his only begotten Son, that whosoever believeth in him should not perish, but have everlasting life"

(John 3:16). "He that believeth on the Son hath everlasting life: and he that believeth not the Son shall not see life; but the wrath of God abideth on him" (John 3:36). If an individual wants to partake of the bountiful love of God, he must receive it through His Son Jesus Christ.

Another misrepresentation of God today is to picture a *God of all goodness,* a divine Santa Claus in the sky, desiring to drop promotion, success, and wealth upon all those who trust Him. Indeed, God does give His children such material blessings, for the Bible says, "Every good gift and every perfect gift is from above" (Jas. 1:17). But He does not manifest His goodness at the expense of His other attributes: His sovereignty. His wisdom, and His justice. Since these are present in every one of His actions, God sometimes includes demotion as well as promotion in His plan: "For promotion cometh neither from the east, nor from the west, nor from the south. But God is the judge: he putteth down one, and setteth up another" (Ps. 75:6,7). We love the last part of the statement, always hoping that we will be the ones whom God "setteth up"; while He sets up one, however, He may also put down another. And sometimes the one He puts down is a Christian.

Some people create in their minds a *God who wants everybody healthy all the time.* Worshiping such a God requires one to ignore a major portion of Scripture, including the following, "No man should be moved by these afflictions: for yourselves know that we are appointed thereunto" (1 Thess. 3:3). Sometimes God can accomplish more through life's afflictions than He can through life's ease. Someone has aptly said, "Afflictions are often God's best blessings in disguise."

We intellectuals of the Western world tend to look with compassion upon primitive tribes whose natives carve gods to their liking. As we study their cultures, we learn that often they cover their carvings with gold to give them immortality.

Then they bow down and worship their creations. When we read of such activities, we wonder how anyone, regardless of his lack of education, could worship a personally-fashioned image and think that it is bigger than he is. But essentially we "enlightened" Christians do the very same thing. We carve our god in our minds and, like the heathen idols, he is too small; he meets our specifications; but he will not stand the test of time; he cannot help in time of need. Sad, isn't it?

We must return to the God of the Scriptures, the God of the ages. A God whose every attribute is in His every action—a God of holiness, truth, justice, mercy, wisdom, goodness, grace, longsuffering, and sovereignty.

Diagramed for easy learning, God's attributes might look like a daisy (see fig. 1; I leave one petal blank to show that the list of attributes is not exhaustive).

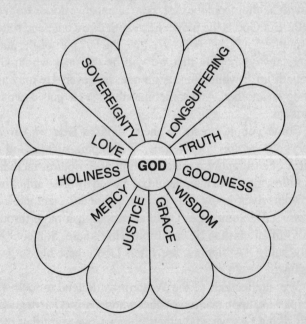

Figure 1

Each petal represents a different attribute of God. If we pluck off one petal, any one of the many, we find ourselves holding a single attribute, a portion of totality, not the whole. This concept of a fragmented deity is abhorrent to those of us who revere God in His holy complexity. Yet it is a concept of many who claim the name of Christian.

God is a God of love, but He is also a God of holiness. God is a God of mercy, but also a God of justice. God controls success; He also controls failure. God triumphs in health; He can also triumph in sickness. Every facet of His character is in every action He takes. Simply, He is God.

On the cross of Calvary we behold this total God in total action. His *sovereignty* formulates the plan of redemption. His *wisdom* sees its final outcome. His *longsuffering* waits for its execution in time. At a predetermined moment in history, His *wrath* descends upon His Son. His *justice* is satisfied with the payment of blood. His *truth* is vindicated with Satan's defeat. His *holiness* is exalted to the heavens. His *mercy* reaches finite men, lost in their darkness of sin. His *grace* gives them faith to trust Him. His *love* shelters them from His anger. His *goodness* abounds in their lives. His total being accomplishes His total purposes. Hallelujah! What a Saviour!

How do you react to this teaching on the nature of God? Recollecting my own rebellious thoughts as a new Christian, I remember how violently I fought God's sovereignty! How I questioned His fairness, His justice, His love! How I finally came to the point of submission where I threw my hands to the heavens and exclaimed, "OK, Lord, you are the Sovereign. I am your subject. You have a right to my life. I give it to you now. You can do anything with me that you want." When I finished my declaration of unconditional surrender, I was at peace. Relief flooded my soul. I knew that I was in the care of the almighty One, then and forever. It was at that point that God began to use me in His service.

My husband is entirely different from me. After almost 20

years of marriage, he exhibits the same quiet spirit that tempered my rebellion during our early years together. He is a trusting man, very teachable, always ready to accept God's Word no matter how hard its admonitions prove to be. I, in contrast, question everything. As I look at him, I wonder how God could take two such totally opposite personalities and make them one in Him. But I know that He is doing exactly that and is doing it beautifully. For we two are cooperating in the teaching of His Word.

As I consider our own different reactions to the Word of God, I fully expect that those same two reactions will be present in you. Some of you will rebel, questioning everything you read. I will identify with your struggle. Others will readily embrace the truth as "harts panting for the water brooks" (see Ps. 42:1). You will be the easy ones to teach. But everyone with a true desire to know God will be fed from His Word. I am assured of that outcome. For God says, "So shall my word be that goeth forth out of my mouth: it shall not return unto me void, but it shall accomplish that which I please, and it shall prosper in the thing whereto I sent it" (Isa. 55:11).

2. The King of Kings

Several years ago, Lee and I taught a class of very sharp young married couples. We imparted to them the same truth that we impart to every class we teach: God is sovereign in the lives of men. We examined His sovereignty in creation, proceeded with His sovereignty in history, and looked with detail at His sovereignty in salvation. The entire course took a year to cover. We ended with a challenge to the students that if they would surrender their lives daily to the will of the King of kings, no limit could be placed upon their spiritual victory.

Then we said to them, "OK, you've sat for a year in a course entitled 'The Sovereignty of God.' Now define God's sovereignty." I will never forget the statement that came from Tom, a doctoral candidate in the field of physics. Although he had not anticipated the question, he was thoroughly prepared for the answer. He said, "The sovereignty of God means that God can do any thing He wants to do, any time He wants to do it, any way He wants to do it, for any purpose He wants to accomplish."

As Tom was completing the last phrase, a hush fell over the room. The simple clarity of his definition had ushered us briefly into God's holy of holies. Lee and I scrambled to add something more theological to his statement, but there was nothing more to add. We both realized that although we had spent many hours of our Christian lives poring over theological treatises and doctrinal discourses, we had never read anything so beautifully simple as Tom's brief statement. Its eloquence quieted us before our Creator.

From that moment on, Tom's definition became an integral part of our teaching. *God can do any thing He wants to do, any time He wants to do it, any way He wants to do it, for any purpose He wants to accomplish.* Who is this God I'm trying to serve? A totally sovereign God.

He says of Himself, "But our God is in the heavens, he hath done whatsoever he hath pleased" (Ps. 115:3). He adds in another Old Testament Scripture, "He doeth according to his will in the army of heaven, and among the inhabitants of the earth, and none can stay His hand, or say unto him, What doest Thou?" (Dan. 4:35). Then in the beautiful book of Ephesians, He affirms that He "worketh all things after the counsel of his own will" (1:11).

Notice the words "all things." Evidently, this comprehensive term includes crises too. God works crises after the counsel of His own will. It is an exciting idea to be sure, but one laden with problems.

Is God the author of evil? Absolutely not. But He is the author of how evil is used. Sometimes He directly sends it, as He did with the plagues in Moses's time. Other times He allows Satan to send it, as He did with Job's crises. Still other times He lets the evil that already exists in the world as a result of Adam's fall touch the lives of certain individuals. However, no matter what the channel is through which evil reaches us, we Christians can be sure of one thing: God will use the evil. He will work it "after the counsel of His own will." The will of God in evil is the same as it is in good—to bring glory to Himself and to benefit His children.

Down through the corridors of history there has been a parade of political leaders who rose up against God and His people. Yet God has moved through these evil men to accomplish holy purposes. His kingship is absolutely without any earthly equal.

First there was Pharaoh of Egypt, shaking his fist at the God of the Israelites. "I refuse to let God's people go!" he said to Moses, asserting his self-inflated sovereignty.

Then the King of kings whispered back from heaven, "Oh, you'll let my people go, mighty Pharaoh, but not until it's my perfect timing. The retention and release of my people is in *my* control, not yours. Furthermore, just so you don't get carried away with the amount of power you have, I want you to know that 'for this cause I have raised thee up, for to show in thee *my* power' " (see Exod. 9:16).

Next came King Nebuchadnezzar of Babylon. "Every knee shall bow to me," he proclaimed, flaunting his supposed authority.

"Not so," said the King of kings from His throne. "I have some servants whose knees will not bow to you. Consider Shadrach, Meshach, and Abednego. Go ahead, test them and see. They will bow only to *me*. Furthermore, I want you to know that a day is coming when *every* knee shall bow to me. And that includes yours, Nebuchadnezzar."

Pilate of Judea was another ruler who got puffed up with the importance of his position. Confronting the Christ who had made him and who, at that very moment was giving him the breath to speak, he asked, "Knowest thou not that I have power to crucify thee or power to release thee?" (see John 19:10). What a question!

"Thou couldst have no power at all against me, except it were given thee from above" (John 19:11), Jesus replied. The answer was a perfect squelch.

To bring us up to date, consider Hitler, a modern example of a tyrant whose evil devices were used by the mighty King of kings. Playing God one day, Hitler announced, "I will eradicate the Jews."

"No," replied the real God, who had called out the Jews for His own special people. "No, you will not eradicate the Jews. I will eradicate you. The Jews will endure forever."

Then the Lord took the terrible atrocities that Hitler committed against His chosen nation Israel to inflame the world's sentiments to such a degree that Israel was granted its original homeland in Palestine, thus fulfilling a prophecy that God had given His people hundreds of years before. A more amazing example of God's sovereignty cannot be found anywhere.

God does use evil for His glory. And God does use evil for His children's good. Perhaps an example of this phenomenon that is dearest to our hearts is the crucifixion of Jesus Christ. The cross was a crisis in the family of God. A planned crisis, to be sure, but a crisis nevertheless. There God's Son was slain by desperately "wicked hands." But at the same time He was "delivered by the determinate counsel and foreknowledge of God." God received the glory, and man received the good, for death was "swallowed up in victory."

If God can take situations so evil as Pharaoh's stubborn rebellion, Nebuchadnezzar's command for self-worship, Pilate's inflated sense of power, Hitler's attempt to arrive at a "final solution" to his problems, and the crucifixion of the Son of God Himself and turn them into some of the greatest blessings the world has ever known, isn't it possible that He might be able to do the same thing with our present family crises? After all, He is the King of kings.

3. The First Cause of Action

Theology names God as the "primary cause of all action." The Westminster Confession of Faith states that "God did ordain whatsoever comes to pass." He usually does not move, however, without secondary causes, which we laymen call "means." Some means which God employs are nature, circumstances, man, Scripture, prayer, the Holy Spirit, and Satan. In figure 2, one block is blank to indicate that the list of means God uses could go on and on. When God moves directly, without ordinary means, we call these events "miracles."

God has the power to turn any action, no matter how evil, to His own glory and to His believers' good. Only believers in Jesus Christ, however, can expect God to move through crises to their benefit. While it is true that God sometimes uses trouble to draw nonbelievers to Himself, it is also true that crises become a source of frustration, despair, and defeat to those who refuse to turn their lives over to God's control.

Let's consider, one by one, the means God uses to accomplish His holy purposes. The first one in figure 2 is that *God moves through nature*. Remember the flood that engulfed the earth but buoyed Noah's family to safety? (See Gen. 6—8.) Here is an example of the same event being used for two different purposes: the destruction of those who rejected God and the salvation of those who trusted Him.

Primary Cause	Secondary Causes (Means)	Results	Example
God	Nature	Glory Good	Flood
God	Circum- stances	Glory Good	Joseph
God	Man	Glory Good	Abraham
God	Word	Glory Good	Eunuch
God	Prayer	Glory Good	Moses
God	Spirit	Glory Good	Pentecost
God	Satan	Glory Good	Job
God		Glory Good	
God	Directly	Glory Good	Miracles

Figure 2

God also moves through circumstances. He allowed Joseph's brothers to sell him into Egypt in order to protect His newly-formed nation of Israel from death by famine (see

Gen. 37). This is an example of evil being turned to good.

Sometimes *God influences men* to carry out His designs. Abraham was His choice to establish the Hebrew nation and to bless the multitude of believers that would eventually come from his seed (see Gen. 12). Those of us who are Christians today can trace our spiritual lineage directly back to Abraham, the patriarch of our faith.

God honors and uses His Word. An Ethiopian eunuch, riding in his chariot one day, found himself wrestling with Scriptures that he did not understand (see Acts 8:26-40). Then Philip, miraculously transported to the scene by a supernatural act of God, enlightened the confused rider. In no time at all, Philip had introduced the eunuch to Christ. Isn't it marvelous to see that God is not limited to moving through only one means at a time? Usually, there are many means being employed in any one particular situation. In this case, God's Spirit moved through Philip, who explained the Scriptures, which in turn affected the eunuch's salvation.

God also utilizes prayer to turn circumstances to His glory, for He is the one who burdens men to pray. The intercession of Moses saved Israel from God's consuming anger (see Exod. 32:9-14). Through prayer Hezekiah gained 15 years of life (see 2 Kings 20:1-6). By petitioning God, Hannah became a mother (see 1 Sam. 1:1-20). The Bible is filled with example after example of effectual prayer.

An equally effective means God uses is the *direct intervention of His Holy Spirit*. At Pentecost He moved in mighty power, causing everyone present to hear the gospel in his own tongue. What a tremendous impact this phenomenon had on Christ's newly-formed church!

The most fascinating idea of all, however, is that *God can move through Satan*. No matter what evil the prince of demons concocts, God is able to overrule his action, turning it to His own glory and to His believers' good. Job is a perfect example of God's manipulation of Satan. Satan deliberately tempted Job in an effort to destroy his faith. But God used Satan's devices to strengthen Job's faith instead. We can still read the account of Job's triumph today, thousands of years after the testing occurred. What a magnificent example of evil turned to glory by a totally sovereign God!

It really does not matter who or what causes the tragedies of life. What matters is what God intends to do with those tragedies. Good and evil are not equal forces in the universe. God controls Satan and the ultimate outcome of his sin. When a believer belongs to the King of kings and Lord of lords, what happens in his life matters less than how God uses what happens in his life. Victory belongs to Christians. It is part of being "joint-heirs with Christ" (Rom. 8:17).

Let's summarize our conclusions thus far: God is in control of everything that happens, crises too. God moves through many means, even Satan, turning evil to ultimate good. Our responsibility as children of His is to trust Him even when the way seems dark. For God's way is always perfect.

Sharing with several different classes this chart on how God moves, Lee and I have had varied reactions, all good. One lady told us that many questions which she had been "harboring for ages" were answered clearly and simply. Another woman came bursting through the classroom door to share how she had "witnessed" to someone in the hospital. "I could see the whole chart before me," she said, "especially those words 'God's glory, His believers' good.' I was absolutely triumphant in my approach." As she continued to share her personal victory, those of us around her paused to thank God that He had chosen to move in our class, even through the likes of us. Now we hope this chapter has cleared up some of your questions too.

4. A Master of Creativity

In order to have victory in the midst of crises, we must get our eyes off the brethren and on the King of kings. When we look at each other, we wonder: Why is that guy receiving so many blessings and I'm not? How come God healed her and I'm still suffering? How can that couple breeze through life so easily and I have so many problems?

Although it may appear that way, nobody goes through life without troubles. Everybody hurts somewhere, either in a major way or in a very small annoying way. God is absolutely creative in His dealings with these hurts. He never treats any two individuals in exactly the same manner: His ways are not our ways; His thoughts are higher than our thoughts (see Isa. 55:8). Because God's motives are lofty, we may not always comprehend the meaning of His actions. Nowhere in Scripture does He command us to *understand* Him; instead, He commands us to *trust* Him. There is a tremendous difference.

Consider the following examples of divine creativity: God healed Hezekiah, but He smote Miriam with leprosy; God raised Lazarus from the dead, but He struck down Ananias and Sapphira; God delivered Paul from prison, but He let John the Baptist remain there and eventually lose his head; God shut the lions' mouths for Daniel, but He made no move to shut them for the early Christian martyrs; God protected Shadrach, Meshach and Abednego from fire, but He let Polycarp burn at the stake; God delivered Jonah from the sea, but He has held back deliverance for other drowning Christians. God gives most people their babies one at a time, but He gave us ours in duplicate.

Any of you parents of twins can probably attest to the fact that sending twins is undisputedly a sovereign act of God, and receiving them a family crisis. Lee and I recollect, with dismay, the days of double formulas, double strollers, and double toilet training—days through which we were too busy to see that blessings can be "double" too. But we did manage to survive our trial. And now we wouldn't trade our "mirror images" for anything in the world.

Read the eleventh chapter of the book of Hebrews and thrill anew at God's creative dealings with His own. Here we learn that Enoch was "translated" without seeing death and we recall that Elijah received a similar "translation." Probably most of us Christians living today are hoping that we too will be listed with those whom God chooses to escape dying. For we know that at the time of Christ's return there will be a gathering up of all living believers, body and soul together (see 1 Thess. 4:17). In other words, there will be no death. This is a blessed expectation, to be sure, but not necessarily a valid one for all of us. Realistically speaking, we have to agree that most of us reading this book should probably expect to die.

But enough of morbid conjecture. Let's think about life instead. Are you smiling with me as we read of Sarah's appalling predicament? Because she was Abraham's wife, she found herself pregnant at the ripe old age of 90 (see Gen. 17:17; 21:1,2). What misery! What pain! What explanations! And we think we're too old when we find ourselves pregnant at 40! What if God decided to repeat the miracle and made us able to conceive children at Sarah's age? Let me guess that all of you women reading this (and probably a few men too) are hoping that this is one miracle that God will choose *not* to repeat. Am I right?

God is as creative in granting victory in battle as He is in bestowing babies. Notice that the walls of the city Jericho fell without the use of any weapons. Is there any other city you can think of, though, that was taken in exactly the same way? See how Rahab was protected because she had hidden God's children? But think of the modern-day heroes and heroines who have also hidden God's children and have *not* been spared.

Look at the phrases in Hebrews 11 that show triumph: "subdued kingdoms, wrought righteousness, obtained promises, stopped the mouths of lions, quenched the violence of fire, escaped the edge of the sword, out of weakness were made strong, waxed valiant in fight, turned to flight the armies of the aliens . . . received their dead raised to life again" (vv. 33,34,35). These phrases belong to "delivered" Christians.

But there are others who were not so blessed. They are the ones who "were tortured . . . had trial of cruel mockings and scourgings . . . bonds and imprisonment . . . were stoned, they were sawn asunder, were tempted, were slain with the sword: they wandered about in sheepskins and goatskins; being destitute, afflicted, tormented" (Heb. 11:35-37). The point to be grasped here is that delivered and nondelivered Christians *all* have the same Sovereign and Lord. He simply uses their lives in entirely different ways.

In Hebrews 12:2 we are told to look "unto Jesus the author and finisher of our faith." Not unto circumstances. Not unto others. But unto Jesus, "who for the joy that was set before him endured the cross," not enjoying His family crisis one bit. Instead, He despised the shame of the cross, but now He is "set down at the right hand of the throne of God." The

Lord says to us, "For consider him that endured such contradiction of sinners against himself, lest ye be wearied and faint in your minds" (12:3).

If Jesus endured, we can endure. The object of our trust, however, must be Christ Himself, not life. Situations in life often deteriorate; relationships fray; sickness may lead to death. Crisis may follow crisis, but God is constant, "the same yesterday, today, and forever." When He enters a crisis, He comes with changing power; but it is usually not the crisis that He changes. It is us. He wants to make us stable, like Him, "the same yesterday, today, and forever." Firm in faith, unmovable in trial, regardless of the circumstances involved. Herein lies life's greatest challenge.

Who is this God I'm trying to serve? He is the God of the Scriptures, not the God of my design. He is infinite and great, the King of the universe and the Lord of history. A God who became accessible to the world in Jesus Christ. When I accepted Him as my Lord and Saviour, He became personal to me. He has taken control of my life, entering every circumstance, treating me uniquely and lovingly. I am special to Him. He fashioned me when I was still in my mother's womb (see Ps. 139:16). He says He has every hair of my head numbered (see Matt. 10:30). He cares about my problems.

I must always remember, however, that God does not exist to satisfy my whims. Any good that comes to me as a Christian is a by-product of my salvation, not its end. Its end is to bring God glory. I exist for the Lord, in life's ease and in life's trials. I am expected to glorify Him with my life in the manner He chooses for me. I count it a privilege to serve the living Christ and rest in full assurance that His way for me is perfect, whether I understand it or not. My crises are in His hands. There they become opportunities.

PART II

WHERE IS GOD?

5. A Biblical Crisis

Where is God when we need Him most? Very far away, it seems. We may scream at Him, shake our fists in frustration, cry buckets of tears, and offer our paltry bargains, but He doesn't even care. So it seems.

Did you ever feel as if you were standing in a cave of self-pity and despair? You can see where the waters of His presence have been. But now that your crisis has come, there is only emptiness where once you were full. You have been drained of your inner resources. Furthermore, the tide of God's influence appears to have departed from your life.

Such thoughts are very depressing. They are also very shortsighted. For what we cannot see is that miles away in the center of the ocean of God's limitless resources, our Lord is beginning to turn the tide of our crisis. Then one day, when we least expect divine intervention, the waters of His sufficiency come racing to meet our need. And we stand drenched in the flood of God's love.

Where is God when we need Him most? He is right in the throes of our crises. In fact, whether we realize it or not, He is actively engaged in all of our problems, accomplishing His purposes even through men's opposing designs. That makes Him an exciting God to serve.

Turn to Genesis 37 and read about a humdinger of a family crisis that occurred in Jacob's family. Unfortunately, Jacob favored Joseph over his other sons. He didn't keep quiet about his favoritism either. He openly displayed it. When Joseph received a "coat of many colors" and the other brothers did not, family discontent smoldered. Jealousy caught fire, and Joseph fanned the flame. He shared some of his dreams, in which it appeared that he would someday rule over the other members of his family. In no time at all, the brothers' jealousy had turned into hatred.

One day the brothers decided to kill the family troublemaker; but one of the brothers, Reuben, was hesitant to shed blood. So they agreed to sell Joseph to a passing caravan instead. This decision was about as evil as family decisions can get. Yet in the hands of God it became a blessing. Later, after Joseph had become a ruler in the land of Egypt, he watched his family enter his presence, begging for food. He turned to his brothers in forgiveness and said, "Be not grieved, nor angry with yourselves, that ye sold me hither: for God did send me before you to preserve life" (Gen. 45:5).

How did Joseph feel in the midst of his life-changing crisis? Terrible, I'm sure. Did he ever think that God had forsaken him? Probably several times. He had been taken as a teenager into a country whose customs were different from his. The language was strange to his ears. He longed for a home-cooked meal and an object familiar to his touch. But nothing from home appeared. In time he was thrown into prison for a crime he did not commit. There he was left to die. In all of his trouble, however, the Bible says, "The Lord was with him, and that which he did, the Lord made it to prosper" (Gen. 39:23).

Eventually Joseph was named second-in-command under Pharaoh. In time of severe famine, people from neighboring countries had to come to him to obtain food. Among them were his brothers. As they stood before him, pleading, the dream-prophecy of his youth was fulfilled—his family did indeed bow down to him. But the most important result of that family's crisis was that the people who would become the nation of Israel migrated to Egypt where they obtained food, grew in knowledge, and multiplied with increasing strength. Joseph said to his family, "But as for you, ye thought evil against me; but God meant it unto good, to bring to pass, as it is this day, to save much people alive" (Gen. 50:20).

Back up to the pivotal point in this family's crisis: Joseph's sale to the Ishmaelites. Let me pose some questions that Lee and I have asked our classes. I'll also share the typical answers.

Who sold Joseph into Egypt?

"His brothers."

Were they free in their action?

"Absolutely."

Was it an evil action?

"Yes."

Were they responsible for their evil action?

"Yes."

Was their evil turned to good?

"Yes."

How?

"God was in the action."

Do you feel that Joseph's brothers ever considered themselves puppets in the hand of God?

"No."

Why not?

"They felt guilty for what they did. Puppets don't feel guilty."

Let me explain what theologians call "the doctrine of divine concurrence." According to Berkhof in his *Summary of Christian Doctrine,* this doctrine states that, "God works in every act of His creatures, not only in their good but also in their evil acts." It also states that "the same deed is in its entirety both a deed of God and a deed of man."[1]

The phrase "in its entirety" is an interesting one. The minute we accept it, we are, mathematically speaking, dealing with two 100 percents. Thinking big is not new to Christians. When we accept the inspiration of Scriptures, we think in terms of two 100 percents. We believe that Luke wrote his Gospel, using his training and his personality of expression. We also believe that God wrote Luke's Gospel. The book belongs 100 percent to two individuals.

When we accept the deity of Christ, we are also thinking big. We believe that Christ was a man, "yet without sin" (Heb. 4:15). But He was also God, able to perform miracles. To reduce His being to 50-50 (50 percent man and 50 percent God) is to introduce heresy to our theology. He is 100 percent man and 100 percent God.

We stretch our minds to grasp the Trinity. We believe that the Father is 100 percent God, the Son is 100 percent God, and the Spirit is 100 percent God. Yet when we add them all together, we still get only 100 percent God. Interesting, isn't it?

Our conversion experiences work the same way. We often say that we "made a decision" for Christ. But when we turn to the Scriptures, we read that God says, "Ye have not chosen me, but I have chosen you" (John 15:16). Who chose whom? Both chose the other.

Truly God is in every action. The fact that He is, however, does not erase man's responsibility for the sin that he commits. Because man's sin is entirely his own doing, he is entirely responsible for its consequences. Joseph's brothers will have to stand before God and give an account of selling their brother into Egypt.

Perhaps from our point of view God moves backward through time. He determines the end that He wants accomplished, then ordains previous action to accomplish that end.

In the case of Joseph, the end of the action was Israel's migration to Egypt. Perhaps God backed up in time to use the sin of Joseph's brothers to bring about that holy end. It is an interesting and mind-expanding conjecture that leaves us quite provoked in thought. How God implements His plan we may never completely understand, but the fact that He is moving constantly in our lives should bring comfort to all of us, especially in our time of need.

6. A Personal Crisis

Several years ago our whole family faced a crisis. At the time we were going through it, we really couldn't see any good coming from it at all, only evil. Just as Joseph languished helplessly in prison thinking he was forsaken, we felt quite abandoned in our crisis, unaware that God was actively working it for His glory and for our ultimate good. Looking back on the experience now, we are ashamed that we felt neglected because we should have known better. We had been watching God fulfill His promises beautifully in our lives for several years. Spending a certain amount of time feeling forsaken, however, seems to be a normal part of crises. Even Christ Himself experienced abandonment. He exclaimed with depth of emotion, "My God, my God, why hast thou forsaken me?" (Mark 15:34).

Lee begins our story: "Several years ago I resigned my secure position in a large corporation to head the marketing operations of a newly-formed small company. One day the additional funding that we had been anticipating failed to materialize, and all 40 employees, including us officers, were terminated without severance pay.

"I'll never forget that day. I was back home by 10:00 in the morning with my devastating news. All I could think of was our finances. We had taken a second mortgage on our home to support this venture. Now we were deeply in debt with no immediate hope for financial recovery. We were without employment direction. The outlook was gloomy.

"I began immediately to circulate resumes. Within a very

short time four possibilities of employment turned up. We didn't want to make another mistake, so we prayed that God would close three of those four open doors. This way we were fail-safe, we reasoned. We would enter the only door left open and enter it confidently. I interviewed and waited.

"Door number one closed. We praised the Lord. He was answering prayer. Then door number two closed. We again praised the Lord, although it was harder this time. Our first two answers had both been negative. Now I must confess that in our minds we had already picked which door we thought God would have us enter. It was door number three. Our choice was clothed with selfishness because the third door would enable us to stay in Lexington, Massachusetts.

"We couldn't see why God would ever move us from there. We both had Bible studies going, I for men, Peg for women. The studies were multiplying. Even the offshoots were flourishing. I was doing some lay preaching. We were both active in our church, which was on the threshold of becoming one of the strongest evangelical congregations in New England. In short, we were glorifying God with our lives. Why would He move us? He wouldn't. We were sure.

"So when I began my final interview for the third job (after 20 hours of previous interviews, I might add), we expected acceptance. This position, which was an opportunity to return to sales, would enable us to stay in our beloved Lexington. The fourth job, which we refused even to think about, would require a move to Detroit.

"After the interview I called Peg, who was sticking quite close to the phone. 'I didn't get the job,' I said flatly.

" 'Why not?' she asked in disbelief.

" 'They said I was manager material. They said I'd never be satisfied to be a salesman again.'

"Peg had to agree. They knew me as well as she did. But the thought that God had let us down was more than Peg could bear. She dissolved in tears.

"I was quick to come to my wife's rescue. 'Peg,' I reminded her, 'remember how we prayed? We prayed that God would leave only one door open, the right one. He has done that. We've *got* to go through it. It's the only one left.'

" 'But Detroit?' she asked in shock. 'God wants us to go to Detroit?' "

Lee then adds: "Folks, I want you to know that God never makes mistakes. We do, but He doesn't. We have been in your midst for eight years now. We have made some of the most precious friends of our lives. We have personally been strengthened in our faith and have had the joy of seeing all of our children make public professions of their faith, *here in Detroit*. My business has flourished, returning all the financial loss. But the greatest blessing of all has been our ministry, which is many times greater than it was in Massachusetts. My wife is speaking to women's groups all over the country. We are team-teaching several classes like this one. And our booklet and tape outreach astounds even us. At times we find it hard to keep up with the orders that come in.

"While going through the crisis, I could not see the hand of God. But He was with us just as surely as He was with Joseph, strengthening our faith, making us more usable for His service, and bringing much good from our difficulty. Looking back on the situation with my 20-20 spiritual hindsight, I would have to say that it appears that God moved the only way He could have moved. Our wills were too stubborn for His gentle prodding. If He really wanted us here in Detroit—and it appears that He did—He couldn't have gotten us here any other way. It took a crisis to accomplish His will."

Christian, are you going through a crisis right now? Stop a minute to analyze what God might be doing through it. Don't be discouraged if you can't see His ultimate purposes, for it often takes time for the plan of God to unfold before human eyes. The same God who ministered to Joseph is ministering to you. He promises, "I will never leave thee, nor forsake thee" (Heb. 13:5).

Lee and I have written a booklet entitled *God Moves Through Man's Freedom*. In it we explain in diagram form how God lays a railroad track of action. Everybody has one. Man freely moves along his rail to an appointed end; God moves along the other rail to the same end. Man's action may involve sin; God's action is always holy. At times God enters man's life in a direct way through one of the railroad ties, influencing man's decisions. At other times, however, God lets man do his own thing, working that thing to His ultimate glory anyway and to His children's good.

The important point to notice, however, is that both tracks of action always end at the same place. In all the years that we have been studying Scripture, we have never come across one situation where man's line of track stopped short of, or proceeded beyond, God's line. In other words, it is impossible for man to thwart or change the ultimate purposes of God. Forces that are out to destroy God's children become putty in the Sovereign's hand. He superintends all action, good or bad, to the end which He has appointed. Understand this important concept, and spiritual victory will be yours.

God's relationship to Christians can be likened to a daughter's relationship to her father who is president of the country, such as Amy Carter's relationship to Jimmy Carter. As president of the country of which she is a citizen, he controls many policies that affect her. But if she should have a problem that demands his immediate attention, she can run directly into his office and snuggle into his comforting arms. For her sovereign is also her father.

So it is with us. God is our great and holy Sovereign. But He is also our loving heavenly Father. We have access to this love at any time of the day or night. He is ready to help us and willing to listen. But, best of all, He is able to turn sorrow to rejoicing.

7. Universal Crises

When God created the earth, everything He made was beautiful and good (see Gen. 1:31). The atmosphere was clear, the water was pure, and the earth abounded with fruit. But there was no one on earth to enjoy this bounty. So God created man. From the dust of the earth He formed a shell. Then He breathed into this shell the breath of life, "and man became a living soul" (Gen. 2:7).

Can you imagine how exciting it must have been for Adam to see God's creation for the very first time? To see the great variety of trees—some majestic and awesome, reaching for the sky, others short and scrubby, yet quite artistic in their shapes; to touch a delicate daffodil, a frilled yellow trumpet of glory; to watch the quiet rose unfold its brilliance in its perfect time; to marvel at the birds soaring in the open sky—some, like the eagle, looming mightily over his head or, like the humming bird, zipping by him with a whirr of its tiny wings.

Then, when God paraded "every beast of the field" before Adam to be named (Gen. 2:19,20), Adam wondered how any creature could handle a neck as long as a giraffe's or antlers as heavy as a caribou's. He studied the well-defined stripes of the zebra and the black spots of the leopard that seemed to flow from the brush of a master Artist. As God's wonders unfolded day after day, man was very appreciative.

Soon after his creation man realized that he was essentially a spiritual being. He thrilled at the knowledge that he, like the other wonders of God's creative hand, had been made to manifest the glory of his Creator. He relished those precious hours spent walking and talking with his Maker. And he loved the intimacy of communion with the Spirit of the one who gave him life. But the body which housed his spirit was equally precious to him. It seemed to be very intricately made. He had eyes that beheld the colors of the garden and ears that caught the distant calls of the birds. He had a nose that smelled the aroma of flowers and a tongue that tasted the fruit from the trees. His fingers touched the smoothness of a petal and fondled the softness of fertile earth. His feet walked the pathways of wonder. But the thing that intrigued man the most was the fact that every function of his body was in perfect harmony with every other function. How wonderful is God! he thought.

His God indeed was wonderful and, I might add, infinitely wise in His judgments. When He placed man in the peaceful garden of Eden, He gave him free access to everything—everything, that is, except the tree of the knowledge of good and evil. By withholding the fruit from this tree, God was reserving for Himself the right to exert His sovereignty over the lives of all His creation. He wanted the prerogative to determine what might be good or what might be evil for man as he trod the pathway of life. But man wanted everything to be under *his* control. He wanted the freedom to judge what might be the best choice to make at any given point in his life. So he ate the forbidden fruit.

The rift came quickly. Concerning the tree of the knowledge of good and evil, God had said, ''In the day that thou eatest thereof thou shalt surely die'' (Gen. 2:17). But Satan, the father of lies, had whispered, ''Ye shall not surely die'' (3:4). And man chose to believe Satan rather than God.

The minute he ate the fruit, however, he realized that he had been deceived. For the spiritual oneness with his Creator was gone. So were those treasured hours of walking and talking with the One who had made him. Now there was only running and hiding—running and hiding from the verdict that was sure to come from the mouth of a holy Judge.

The body also felt the change. But the bodily change was less obvious to man than the change in his spirit. It took longer to manifest itself. Man had heard God pronounce, "For dust thou art, and unto dust shalt thou return" (Gen. 3:19), but I imagine that man went about his daily routine for several years before he noticed a dimness in his sight or a loss in his once-acute hearing. For the degenerative process of aging manifests itself slowly. And disease invades the body quite silently. But the blight on God's perfect creation was working and would intensify its impact on man as history turned its pages.

Nature fell under a similar curse. God said, "Cursed is the ground . . . Thorns also and thistles shall it bring forth" (Gen. 3:17,18). Where once only productive plants flourished, now weeds proliferated and conquered. Where once the soil was soft and fertile, the desert staked its claim and sapped the life-giving moisture. Mountains spewed their fury into the sea, leaving mute evidence of the pressures mounting deep within the heart of the earth. Shifting of the continental plates tore land masses in half, then covered their shores with the floods of giant waves. The whole earth groaned within itself, waiting for release from its curse.

Satan himself, the catalyst for all those negative happenings, also was cursed. God said, "Because thou hast done this, thou art cursed above all cattle, and above every beast of the field; upon thy belly shalt thou go, and dust shalt thou eat all the days of thy life" (Gen. 3:14). From that moment on, Satan was to be a defeated foe, groveling in corruption, awaiting final punishment.

Meanwhile, man, now possessing the knowledge of good and evil, determined the course that his life on earth should take. But his limited understanding of the scope of creation's curse soon led him to make fatal decisions. In an effort to "get while the getting's good," he polluted his skies, contaminated his streams, and over-farmed the fields God had given him. He satisfied his own desires by taking into his body harmful substances and saturating his mind with the lusts of his flesh. Gone was the purpose of glorifying God. In its place was sheer survival. He spent a great portion of his life struggling to cope with the problems that he himself had introduced to the universe. He still does.

Without the enlightenment of the Spirit of God, man will never acknowledge that sin is the cause of his problems. He will try by his own efforts to extricate himself. Unfortunately, most of his solutions are either temporary or abortive. For example, he invents religion to elevate his spirit, but the legalism that accompanies it sends him sinking in despair. He invests in medical technology to prolong the life of his body but his body dies anyway, sometimes from quite insignificant causes. He approves conservation of natural resources to replenish the world's supplies, but he wastes fuel and water in his own home with scarcely a thought for the rest of mankind.

Man is powerless to help himself eternally. The sooner he comes to this realization, the better. For God, not man, is sovereign over all. Only God can eradicate sin. Only God can give eternal life. And only God can initiate salvation. It is He who enlightens man's mind, both to see the scope of man's dilemma in sin and the efficacy of God's solution in Christ. For in His Son lies man's redemption. Total. Everlasting. And free.

On the cross of Calvary, Jesus Christ took action to restore His precious creation to its original condition. Being free from sin Himself, He died a sinner's death "to reconcile all things unto himself" (Col. 1:20). This comprehensive statement means that in His death was redemption for man's spirit, redemption for man's body, and redemption for the rest of God's creation.

Most of the preaching that we hear today deals with the redemption of man's spirit and rightly so, because, of the areas in life that sin has touched, it is the only one that has eternal value. But the house for the spirit, the body, was also included in Christ's atoning work. When He arose from the grave in power in the same body in which He had died, He was showing the world that He had conquered death, the body's greatest enemy. He was also promising us that some-day, at the resurrection of believers, we too would receive glorified bodies, every bit as victorious as Christ's body.

It is interesting to note that while Christ was dying, He wore a crown of thorns upon His brow. This crown indicates that nature itself was not forgotten in His amazing redemptive work. He intended that someday "instead of the thorn shall come up the fir tree" (Isa. 55:13). Indeed it will, as a final manifestation of Christ's redemption of His world. But this restoration of nature will not occur until God's predetermined timetable so decrees. For His plan for the earth unfolds progressively.

At the cross the price of redemption was paid in full for every area affected by sin. But only a restored spirit is available to the believer now. In the plan of God there will be a future delivery of man's restored body and eventual harmony in the rest of God's creation. To illustrate the situation, I offer the following analogy: suppose I go into a department store and select items of furniture that I need. That day I pay in full for all three things I buy—a sofa, a chair, and a rug. When I go to pick them up, the clerk tells me that only the sofa is in stock. I can take it home today if I want to, he says. But I will have to wait a while for the other two purchases I made. The clerk assures me that the chair should arrive in about a week. The rug, in about a month. Being an impatient person, I know that I will have a hard time waiting, but at no time during the delay do I have any doubt that my purchases are coming. I completely trust the store.

So it is with salvation. When we come to a point of personal commitment of our lives to Christ, a miracle occurs within. We immediately receive the redemption of our spirits; our sins are forgiven; our guilt is gone. And for the first time in our lives we are at peace with God. We have been "born again" into His family. This is where Romans 8:16,17 begins: "The Spirit itself beareth witness with our spirit, that we are the children of God: and if children, then heirs; heirs of God, and joint-heirs with Christ; if so be that we suffer with him, that we may be also glorified together."

Then God goes on to explain His timetable for the redemption of the body and for the rest of creation. He says that nature has to wait until last for its restoration. It follows "the manifestation of the sons of God" (Rom. 8:19), a phrase which most commentators feel refers to the resurrection of the body. Meanwhile, nature "groans and travails in pain" (see v. 22). It endures earthquakes, volcanoes, tidal waves, hurricanes, tornadoes, and other devastating calamities.

The non-Christian, devoid of a reconciled spirit, has a hard time living in his unreconciled world. But so does the Christian—in fact, his predicament is intensified. For his spirit has been restored, but the body which houses it has not. God says that we who "have the firstfruits of the Spirit . . . groan within ourselves, waiting for the adoption, to wit, the redemption of our body" (v. 23). Not only that, but we are waiting for the redemption of our world as well. No wonder crises bother us! In a sense, we may be more acutely aware of their intrusions than the non-Christian is. But there is one important difference between us and him: We have Christ the victor living within; the non-Christian has nothing.

Why doesn't God speed up His redemptive timetable? Why does He make us wait until the future resurrection to receive perfect, pain-free houses for our spirits? Well, simply speaking, the waiting brings Him glory. He deals with it creatively, uniquely tailoring His actions to meet the needs of individuals. Sometimes He performs miracles and heals disease-ridden bodies. When He does so, the healings are an earnest pledge of what He will do perfectly, someday. At best, however, these healings are temporary. So God usually withholds the spectacular in favor of performing the effectual. In other words, God chooses the greater miracle, not of taking the suffering away, but of giving the Christian victory *in the midst* of his suffering.

God's persistent purpose throughout the lives of his saints is to conform us "to the image of his Son" (v. 29). He wants us to become patient, enduring, God-glorifying Christians. But such a remodeling job takes time. And the period of transition breeds concern. So while we are struggling with our doubts, the Saviour comes to our aid with His love. He says, "I will cover every tendency to fail that you might have. Even when you come to the end of yourself and don't know how to pray as you ought (a new home or not? promotion or not? healing or not?); even then, I will be there, right in the middle of your crisis. I will send my Holy Spirit to pray for you 'with groanings which cannot be uttered' " (see v. 26). This will be a silent but effectual prayer. For the Spirit of God prays "according to the will of God" (v. 27). When we surrender our prayer life in this manner to the Lord, we give up demanding Him to do our selfish bidding. Instead, we yield ourselves to Him—body, soul, and desires—to accomplish *His* perfect will.

8. Precious Promises

"I'll see you on Friday," Lee used to say. My soul would reach out for every word. That was a very precious promise to me. It would enable me to get through the week ahead, day by day. Monday was always hard for me because the pangs of separation were still very strong. Tuesday I would begin to recover from my loss. Then on Wednesday I would mark the halfway point. By Thursday I would begin to get excited. And by the time Friday morning rolled around, I could hardly contain myself. My fiancé would at last be coming back.

Such was the pattern for our lives the year Lee and I were engaged to be married. While he was serving in the United States Army, stationed in Virginia, I was teaching school in New Jersey. Both of us were miserable a good part of the time. For even though we loved each other dearly and desperately wanted to consummate that love, we felt we should fulfill our personal obligations before we got married. To do so, we had to be separated.

The most precious gift we had while we were absent from each other were the promises made when we had been together. They weren't as good as having each other. But they were enough. They got us through the hard places and gave us hope for the future.

Everybody likes to receive promises, especially when

those promises come from someone trustworthy. They give hope in the midst of despair. They are lights at the end of the tunnels of our lives. They give an optimistic attitude even in the most pessimistic situations of life. They sustain us.

We Christians are especially blessed in this regard. We have been given promises by the faithful Creator Himself. Those promises enable us to keep going when we can no longer see the way because we know that someday, somehow they will be fulfilled. God says so. We might not know how and we often don't know when. But we do know the One who is doing the promising, and that should be good enough for all of us.

God has some precious promises to offer those caught in the crises of life.

The first promise is thrilling. It states that *"all things work together for good to them that love God,* to them who are the called according to his purpose" (Rom. 8:28). At the end of a class in which we shared this promise, one of my friends, who had recently lost a young child, shared how blessed she was to come to the realization that the things which happen to Christians are not necessarily good in themselves, but all together they combine to make good. The things which happened to Jacob's son, Joseph, caused the old patriarch to sigh, "All these things are against me" (Gen. 42:36). But in the hands of God those very same things which individually were against him worked together for his benefit. This promise is given to Christians only. All things do not necessarily work together for good for one who is outside of Christ.

God's second promise in the midst of crises is that *He will finish what He has begun in our lives.* No matter how small our faith may be, God will nourish it until it grows to the size which He desires. The Bible says, "For whom he did foreknow, he also did predestinate to be conformed to the image of his son . . . . Moreover, whom he did predestinate, them he also called: and whom he called, them he also

justified: and whom he justified, them he also glorified''
(Rom. 8:29,30). God puts the last verb in the past tense even
though it has not yet happened in our experience. In the mind
of God the plan formulated is just as good as the plan accomplished. We *will* someday be glorified because God com-
pletes every work which He begins.

Another promise that God makes is to *intercede for us
when we're having problems*. This truth makes Paul exclaim,
''If God be for us, who can be against us?'' (8:31). When we
realize that few men have endured more crises in life than
Paul did, we come to appreciate the triumph in his theology.
He was beaten, stoned, robbed, shipwrecked, and impris-
oned. Yet he considered himself to be on the winning side.

Not only does God affirm that He will act on our behalf,
but He actually promises *to give us victory in the midst of our
crises*. Paul says, ''In all these things we are more than
conquerors through him that loved us'' (8:37). When we are
beset by enemies on every side, whether they be real or
imagined, we tend to cling to any encouraging word, especially one that comes from the Lord Himself. We readily
grasp the concept of conquering. We know that to take a job
after a period of unemployment is to conquer, even if the job
lasts only temporarily. To become resigned to the death of a
spouse is to conquer, even though we may still have to
overcome moments of overwhelming depression. To receive
physical healing is to conquer, even though we know that we
will get sick again and eventually die. But what does it mean
to be *''more* than a conqueror''? Perhaps it means to go on
with Christ in glory, where conditions are permanent, not
temporary. Perhaps that is why ''the others'' in Hebrews 11
did not accept deliverance. They were looking for a ''better
resurrection'' (Heb. 11:35).

Whether our victory lies on earth or in heaven, we are
assured of one final promise: *God will keep us in His love*.
The Scripture says: ''Who shall separate us from the love of

Christ? shall tribulation, or distress, or persecution, or famine, or nakedness, or peril, or sword? . . . I am persuaded, that neither death, nor life, nor angels, nor principalities, nor powers, nor things present, nor things to come. Nor height, nor depth, nor any other creature, shall be able to separate us from the love of God, which is in Christ Jesus our Lord'' (Rom. 8:35-39).

Try to picture in your mind a loved one who has gone on to glory. (Once as I was making this statement, I caught the glance of a mother who was still recovering from the death of her adult son. She was clinging to every word.) What would that saint say if he could speak to us tonight? How would he view the crisis that took him home to his place in eternal glory? Would he consider himself a conqueror? Would he, in any way, be *"more* than a conqueror"?

I personally have never heard from anyone who has passed on to glory—not anyone except Christ, that is. And He said, "Eye hath not seen, nor ear heard, neither have entered into the heart of man, the things which God hath prepared for them that love him" (1 Cor. 2:9). But my husband and I did receive a letter from someone who died a few hours after he wrote the letter. By the time we received it, it seemed as if it were a direct communication from eternity. The letter came from Tom, the boyfriend of a new girl in our Sunday School class. Tom, in his early twenties, was dying from cancer. Brenda asked us to pray for him. We did. The following is part of what Tom wrote to us right before he died:

> *I would like to thank you for praying for me in this time of need. It's been wonderful to know that there are Christian brothers and sisters praying for me who don't even know me. I feel my time here on earth is coming to a close. And I am truly looking forward to that moment when I will be with Him at last. One thing though, Brenda is the greatest friend I have and*

a friend like her doesn't come easily. I just can't see heaven being heaven without her or people like you two. I know it's been a misfortune for me in not meeting you, but I'm truly looking forward to meeting you all in heaven. Just think of what a family reunion that will be . . .

From this short deathbed communication, the gamut of emotions that Tom must have experienced cannot possibly be fully appreciated. Yet his attitudes toward life and death can be. Is there any hint that he begrudged Brenda her health? Was he bitter toward God for his misfortune? Or was he "more than a conqueror" through the Lord of life and death? Perhaps these are some of the questions that God keeps to Himself with answers unrevealed for the purpose of making our desire for heaven a little more intense.

PART III

WHY MUST WE HAVE CRISES?

9. Snakes and Lions

Why are there crises in my life? Although there are many answers to this nagging question, none of those answers really satisfy. Imagine, if you can, that God has personally told you why your particular trial has entered your life. After hearing the answer, even if it is the ultimate answer, are you satisfied? I suspect not. No answer given on this earth will quiet every doubt. Perhaps this is why God keeps the ultimate answer to Himself, at least for now. Christ told His disciples, "I have yet many things to say unto you, but ye cannot bear them now" (John 16:12).

There are several superficial answers to the question "Why?" One is obvious. There are crises in our lives because we are members of the human race.

Let me ask you a question. *Does the fact that you are a Christian necessarily remove you from crises?*

No. Christians, as well as non-Christians, are part of life's statistics. Christians die of heart attacks. Christians get cancer. Christians have accidents. Christians perish in war.

Now let me pose a more difficult question. *Does the fact that you are a Christian* **ever** *remove you from life's crises?*

It could. At a particular time in the history of God's children, the Israelites, He spared them trials that affect most people. Sickness was one of these trials. He said to them, "If thou wilt diligently hearken to the voice of the Lord thy God, and wilt do that which is right in his sight, and wilt give ear to his commandments, and keep all his statutes, I will put none of these diseases upon thee, which I have brought upon the

Egyptians: for I am the Lord that healeth thee'' (Exod. 15:26). As they trekked through the wilderness, the Hebrews were even protected from the usual deterioration of aging clothes. The Bible says that for 40 years, ''their clothes waxed not old, and their feet swelled not'' (Neh. 9:21).

Other children of God have been similarly blessed. Enoch escaped death. Paul was protected from snakebite. And several Israelite leaders were saved from the wounds of battle. God meets unique situations in unique ways.

Perhaps you are wishing that God would repeat some of these miracles for you, especially the one concerning the swelling feet. Although He could, He probably will not. For sickness, death, snakebites, battle wounds, fraying clothes, and swelling feet are all part of life. God has never protected anybody from *all* of these problems.

So then, *what is it that determines whether a Christian goes through a crisis or escapes a crisis?* The answer is obvious. It is the sovereignty of God.

At this point let me deal with a problem that bothers many Christians: When do I apply the promises of God? Are they all for me? Can I claim them any time I want to?

The whole Bible is indeed written for all of us. God says, ''All scripture is given by inspiration of God, and is profitable for doctrine, for reproof, for correction, for instruction in righteousness: that the man of God may be perfect, thoroughly furnished unto all good works'' (2 Tim. 3:16,17). If we are ''men of God,'' then all Scripture is written for us.

There are, however, both universal promises and specific promises contained in the Word of God. The universal promises can be applied to *all* Christians *all* of the time. Ephesians 1:11 is a universal promise: God works ''all things after the counsel of his own will.'' He *always* does this. Romans 8:28 is another universal promise, ''All things work together for good to them that love God.'' As children of God, we can claim these and other universal promises any time in our lives and expect God to fulfill them for us. However, He reserves the right to fulfill even the universal promises *His* way.

The specific promises in Scripture apply to *some* Christians some of the time. Psalm 91 is one such Scripture. In it God promises, "A thousand shall fall at thy side, and ten thousand at thy right hand; but it shall not come nigh thee" (v. 7). In battle and in natural disasters, *some* Christians have been spared while thousands have fallen around them. But *all* Christians have not been spared. And some Christians who have escaped once, may not necessarily escape a second time. God is sovereign in His application of the promise.

The psalm also includes the promise, "Neither shall any plague come nigh thy dwelling" (v. 10). Sometimes God allows an individual to minister to hundreds of sick people without contracting the disease himself. Other times the individual falls with the multitudes. God probably gave this promise to the psalm writer himself, who watched God apply it to his own life. God is absolutely sovereign as to whether or not He chooses to repeat the promise today.

A phrase in the psalm that has been wrested from its context by a cult of snake-treading zealots is the following: "Thou shalt tread upon the lion and adder, the young lion and the dragon shalt thou trample under feet" (v. 13). You have probably seen pictures on television of these zealots treading on adders and escaping harm. Can you ever remember seeing, however, a picture of anybody trampling a lion? On the contrary, you probably have vivid pictures in your imagination of early Christian martyrs being trampled *by* lions.

Be careful about pressing God to fulfill this particular promise in your life. You may end up with snakebite. Or lionbite. Or a crushed pelvis. With specific promises, deliverance lies with God's sovereignty. If it is in His plan to apply the promise, He will do so. If it is *not* in His plan to apply the promise, you will reap the consequences of presumptuous prayer.

10. Wrestling with God

In our effort not to be presumptuous by claiming God's promises wrongly, we must remember a balancing truth. God can take any promise—and I mean *any* promise—and apply it to our lives if He wants to. He can even take the snake and lion promise that He gave specifically to men of old and use it in our lives if He desires. What we must be careful of is assuming that He always will. You see, God reserves the right to choose the time and situation to apply His promises meaningfully. When *we* do the choosing, God is under no obligation to cater to our whims. If, on the other hand, we let Him be Lord of His promises, then we can claim them as He gives them and *know* that they will be fulfilled.

Let me explain what I mean by sharing a personal account of another of our own family crises. I have chosen this particular event because the promise that God gave me came from Psalm 91, the abused promise passage. Yet when I received the verses, they were as fresh as if they had been penned just for me.

Our son Greg had been sick for three months, running a fever that frightened me. How sick he was I did not know, for I am not a physician. But I did know that he was getting no better, even though our doctor had been experimenting with most of the antibiotics on the market. One night, when I felt that I could bear the strain of uncertainty no longer, I went to my room alone. There I thought of someone else who had been alone in His crisis—Jesus the Christ—alone in the garden, alone at the trial, alone on the cross. Even though people surrounded Him constantly, He remained alone with His burden. The two of us shared feelings that night.

Then I thought of God the Father. He too was alone. I wondered what He thought in those hours before He was required to give up His Son. Then I thought of my own son. I didn't know if he was sick unto death or not, but I had to come to grips with the fact that he might be. I knew that God had a right to take him. Greg belonged to Him, not to us. My problem was my love. The knowledge of God's sovereignty that I had in my head couldn't find its way to my heart. In those dark and lonely hours of unrest, Jacob of old had nothing on me; I wrestled with the Lord just as he had done many years before. And I was just as determined to win as I am sure he had been. I should have known that when one wrestles with God, he *never* wins. Just before daybreak the battle ended. I told the Lord, ''All right. You win! I give you my son. Now please, just give me your peace.''

He did. At my moment of surrender God spoke, not in an audible voice but in a ''still, small voice'' deep within my soul. ''Read Psalm 91,'' He said. I began. The words fell in their normal order until I came to verses 15 and 16. Then a miracle occurred. Gregory's name appeared in place of the pronouns. This is what I read, ''Greg shall call upon me, and I will answer Greg. I will be with Greg in trouble. I will deliver Greg and honor Greg. With long life will I satisfy Greg and show Greg my salvation.''

I laid down my Bible and sobbed. Then I slept for the first time in several nights. God answered my prayer, and He did it through His Word. Magnificent! I knew that I would carry the memory of that experience into eternity with me, locked with other treasures in my heart. I had been in the holy presence of God, personally encountered, personally uplifted.

Greg recovered from his illness and is a robust teenager today. He has entrusted his life to the One who "showed him His salvation." He has not forgotten his deliverance.

I want to make it very clear that God sovereignly applied that promise to my son's life. He didn't have to. In response to my agony that night, He could have whispered quietly that He was going to take my child to heaven. Then, with countless mothers through the ages, I would have had to bow to His decision. I do believe, however, that if God had chosen to take Greg, He would have given me a different Scripture. Perhaps it would have been, "The Lord gave, and the Lord hath taken away; blessed be the name of the Lord" (Job 1:21). But He decided to spare Greg, so He gave me Psalm 91 instead. What a magnificent God we serve!

11. The Problem of Suffering

Suffering is universal. It affects everyone. As the book of Job says, "Man is born unto trouble, as sparks fly upward" (5:7). Everybody hurts somewhere. Some people hurt in big ways, others hurt in small ways. But all people hurt. Elisabeth Elliott defines suffering as "anything about which one says 'Oh, no!' "[2] I like her comprehensive definition.

It is probably safe to say that all suffering in the world is a result of sin, either directly or indirectly. When God made the world, He created everything good. It was not until sin was introduced that suffering arrived. After Adam disobeyed the Lord's commandment, God said to him, "I will greatly multiply thy sorrow . . . cursed is the ground for thy sake; in sorrow shalt thou eat of it all the days of thy life; in the sweat of thy face shalt thou eat bread . . . for dust thou art, and unto dust shalt thou return" (Gen. 3:16-19).

Most suffering in the world is attributable directly to Adam's sin. We partake of it because we are part of the human race. Now that suffering is in the world, it can come to us through a variety of sources. One of these sources is other human beings. For example, a father with venereal disease may produce a child that is blind. In this case, the child suffers because of his father's sin. A mother who is a heroin addict may give birth to a baby that is forced to battle withdrawal symptoms before it ever leaves the hospital. An alcoholic parent may cause his family untold misery—physical, emotional, and mental—because of his uncontrolled habit. In all of these cases suffering is caused by another human being, specifically a parent. Perhaps these are the types of situations that the Lord was referring to when He said that He visits "the iniquity of the fathers upon the children unto the third and fourth generation" (Num. 14:18).

Suffering, however, can come from sources other than parents. Consider the following incidents: a speeding motorist runs a stoplight and maims an innocent victim for life; a lustful man rapes a young girl, marring her future marriage; a political tyrant plunges his nation into unnecessary war, snatching fathers from children and sons from mothers; a neighbor gossips, ruining a friend's reputation. The list could continue.

Still another source of pain is me. My own sin can cause severe problems both for myself and for those whose lives I touch. If I sin against God I should expect to suffer a breach of fellowship with Him. If I sin against my fellowman I should expect a broken relationship to ensue. When a crisis enters my family because of my own personal sin, I must realize that there can be no mending of torn feelings until I confess that sin both to God and to the people whom I have offended. Although God will forgive confessed sin, He will not necessarily remove its consequences. They are part of His law of cause and effect. They may be with me for the rest of my life. When David sinned with Bathsheba then arranged the death of her husband, his sin loomed ever before him (see Ps. 51:3). He confessed before God with a contrite heart, but his baby died anyway (see 2 Sam. 12:7-18), and Bathsheba's dead husband was not resurrected.

If you have personally precipitated a family crisis or have deliberately added fuel to one that was already smoldering, your primary obligation of the moment is to confess your sin first to God and then to your offended family members. If you are unsure whether or not the fault is yours, it does not hurt to confess anyway. Then and only then can soothing healing begin.

When a sin is premeditated and deliberate, God sometimes moves in immediate judgment. He smote Miriam and Uzziah with leprosy because of their sins of presumption. He struck Ananias and Sapphira with death because of their sin of pretense. Jesus warned the impotent man at the pool of Bethesda to "sin no more, lest a worse thing come unto thee" (John 5:14).

But let us not jump to false conclusions at this point. The man blind from his birth was afflicted neither because of personal sin nor because of the sin of others. Jesus said he was blind that "the works of God should be made manifest in him" (John 9:3). It might behoove us as children of God to remember that "we see through a glass darkly" (1 Cor. 13:12). We do not always know the reason for people's calamities. In any event, we should be less concerned with the cause of a crisis than we are with its outcome. The cause often rests with the counsels of God, but the outcome may rest directly with us. Let's get on with our business of living and leave God's business to Him.

Most suffering in life has no direct link to any personal cause. It is attributable to the general state of sin that has gripped our whole planet. We earth-dwellers are partakers of suffering because suffering is in the world. We get colds from germs in the air. We get high blood pressure from living in stressful situations. We suffer indigestion because we have to bolt our food in order to meet our next appointment. Sometimes we have trouble sleeping at night because there are too many things on our minds. These are problems associated with basic living in the world as it exists today. The list could be extended.

As we have seen in our study so far, some crises in life are direct results of someone's sin. Other crises, however, have nothing whatsoever to do with anyone's sin. Still others can fall into either category, depending on the situation involved. Sickness is one of these crises.

Please pay close attention to this point. I do not want to be misunderstood in this controversial area, but I do want to uphold God's truth in its totality. Most theological errors occur because passages are taken out of their context—not only out of the context of the chapter in which they are written, but out of the context of the Bible as a whole. If we want to understand God's relationship to sickness and healing, we should study every passage dealing with these subjects from Genesis to Revelation. What we will discover is that God is totally sovereign in sickness and totally sovereign in healing. Sometimes He directly sends sickness, other times He lets it come naturally. Sometimes He intervenes in the sickness and heals, other times He lets the patient die. Occasionally He gives explanations for His behavior, usually, however, He lets us wonder. He is God.

12. God's Sovereignty in Healing

Did you ever notice that no matter how many times you cut your finger, it always heals itself? That when you break a bone, it knits back together again? That when you catch a cold, if you wait long enough, you will be just as good as new? Why? Because God has built into the human body a natural healing mechanism.

Aren't you glad that He has? It would be both painful and annoying to have to go through the rest of your life with an arm you broke when you were 12. Or with a cold you caught as a teenager. It is our built-in healing mechanism that gives us optimism no matter how seriously ill we are. We naturally expect to get better.

There are times, however, when people do not get better, when they get worse and worse and then die. Do these times mean that God is any less in control, that things have somehow gotten out of hand?

No indeed. What they mean is that God is exercising His sovereignty in healing. During His visit to our hurting planet, He did not make everybody well. He could have but He didn't. Although there were occasions when He healed all the sick in His presence (see Matt. 9:35), there were other times when He healed "as many as touched Him" (see Matt.

14:35,36). Once He healed two from the entire multitude (see Matt. 20:29-34). And another time He healed only one (see Mark 10:46-52). At least once in Christ's ministry, great multitudes came to be healed "and He withdrew" (Luke 5:16), apparently not healing anybody, at least not at that time.

In the case of His beloved friend Lazarus, Jesus deliberately withheld healing. After Lazarus's death, several of the Jews commented on Jesus' restraint: "Could not this man, which opened the eyes of the blind, have caused that even this man should not have died?" (John 11:37). Indeed, Christ *could* have rescued Lazarus from death; but the stark fact confronts us that He did not. He waited "two days still in the same place where he was" (John 11:6)—two precious days before answering the emergency.

Martha didn't understand Jesus' apparent reluctance to help any better than the Jews did. She cried to Him in anguish, "If thou hadst been here, my brother had not died" (John 11:21). Notice that healing was not withheld because of lack of faith—Martha had ample faith. She knew that Christ could have healed Lazarus if He had wanted to, but He had not wanted to. He had a motive in waiting which His earthbound friends could not see. Lazarus's sickness was to be "not unto death, but for the glory of God, that the Son of God might be glorified thereby" (John 11:4). Healing was withheld because of God's sovereignty. He had a greater miracle planned.

Just as God is sovereign in whom He heals, *He is also sovereign in the methods He employs*. He can heal with medicine or without medicine, gradually or instantaneously, using faith or bypassing it. Let's consider some more examples from the ministry of Christ. Sometimes He touched the ill one, even the repulsive-looking leper (see Matt. 8:3). Other times the sick touched Him, grasping even for the hem of His garment (see Matt. 14:36). Occasionally He asked His patient to do something "impossible," such as stretching forth his withered hand (Mark 3:5). In one Old Testament situation God commanded a military captain to perform a seemingly ridiculous stunt, in this case to wash in a muddy river seven times (see 2 Kings 5:10). But the "stunt" worked. The captain was healed.

Once Christ made clay out of spit and anointed the eyes of a blind man (see John 9:6). Another time He "spit on the eyes" without employing dirt (see Mark 8:23). This particular blind man received his restoration in two stages (see Mark 8:24,25). Most others whom Jesus healed were restored all at once. Sometimes prayer and fasting were used (see Mark 9:29). No matter what method God chose, however, that method was always successful. As gospel singer Ethel Waters used to say, "God don't sponsor no flops."

Many people wonder about the role that faith plays in healing. As with everything else we've studied so far, *God is sovereign in His bestowal of faith*. He is also sovereign in its use. He may choose to use it or not to use it, as He sees fit. He does not need great amounts of man's faith in order to perform a healing. In fact, He doesn't need man's faith at all. The demoniacs were godless individuals, anti-Christ in their attitudes, in their statements, and in their actions. Yet Christ showed compassion and healed them (see Matt. 8:28-34; 17:18).

Most of the time, Christ did heal through faith. But the healing did not always occur through the faith of the sick one. To the woman with the issue of blood He said, "Thy faith hath made thee whole" (Mark 5:34). But when the servant of the centurion became ill, Christ did not even see the sick one. He chose to move through the centurion's faith instead. He remarked to the soldier, "I have not found so great faith, no, not in Israel" (Matt. 8:10). Likewise, when the friends of a palsied man let him down through the roof of a home where Jesus was ministering, "When Jesus saw *their* faith, he said

unto the sick of the palsy, Son, thy sins be forgiven thee . . . .
Arise, and take up thy bed, and go thy way into thine house''
(Mark 2:5,11).

The source of true faith is God, not man. Man cannot
manufacture effectual healing faith, no matter how hard he
tries. Christ is ''the author and finisher of our faith'' (Heb.
12:2). He gives faith as He wills. And He increases faith as
He wills. He is responsible for the amount of faith each
individual receives. The Bible says, ''God hath dealt to every
man the *measure* of faith'' (Rom. 12:3). If God intends to use
faith in healing, it is up to Him to give it.

Although man is not the author of faith, he is certainly the
channel through which it flows. God does not move without
man's cooperation. He expects man to exercise that which he
has been given—no more, no less. Through faith, man makes
God's plan for his life a reality. No matter how much faith a
man has, however, he will have no effect on anything unless
God has planned it that way. Pertaining to healing, man's
faith will cause it to happen only if God has planned that it
happen. If healing is not in God's plan, no amount of faith
will make it occur. To suppose so is a presumption.

There is tremendous harm being done today in the name
of Jesus Christ. The sick are being made to feel guilty. Allow
me to share some statements I hear spoken to people on beds
of affliction. These statements are being made by people who
bear the name ''Christian.'' Yet the effects of their
philosophies are devastating to the ill. I will deal with the
remarks one at a time.

The first one I am hearing is, *You are sick because you've
sinned*. Imagine the Pharisaic attitude of the one who speaks
these words! He must think he's God Himself! Before we
jump to radical conclusions, however, let me point out that in
certain cases the statement could be true. People do sometimes get sick because they have personally sinned. Most of
the time, though, people get sick just because they are human

beings. Sickness has befallen the human race.

Job's friends made a similar remark to him. As we read the account of Job's crisis, the sincere desire of his friends to help him becomes obvious. But so does their mistake. It is possible to be sincerely wrong. Only God can link sickness with sin and be correct every time He does so. Only He knows the reason for all illnesses. We do not. In areas where we have incomplete understanding, it is best to keep our thoughts to ourselves.

The second statement I am hearing is equally distressing: *Healing is in the atonement of Christ. It's part of God's plan for every Christian. You're sick because you're not claiming victory.* This series of sentences is particularly deceiving because it contains partial truth. Unfortunately, the sick person may hear only the error and be too weak to combat it.

It is true that the redemption of the body, as well as the redemption of the spirit, was covered in the atonement of Christ. The Scripture says, "But he was wounded for our transgressions, he was bruised for our iniquities: the chastisement of our peace was upon him; and with his stripes we are healed" (Isa. 53:5). Although the context of this passage refers primarily to spiritual healing—the salvation of the soul, it could also be interpreted to include physical healing as well. For the power to perform all healing issues from Christ's triumph over death. But, as we have already learned, the timetable for delivery of perfect bodies is different from that of perfect spirits. Perfect healing of the body comes at resurrection; that's when every Christian will be made totally whole. Any healing before that is strictly a firstfruit of the glorious harvest that will follow. Responsibility for perfection does not lie with the sinner, it lies with the Sovereign. We creatures of God don't dictate to the Creator what to do and when to do it. The great Creator dictates to us what to do and when to do it.

The third statement I often hear is a humiliating one: *You don't have enough faith. If you did, you could walk out of this hospital right now.* Ridiculous. Faith does not determine health. If it did, why aren't all Christians healthy and all non-Christians sick? God's sovereignty determines health. He allows some of His most precious saints to suffer terrible affliction. He gives them faith to endure, no matter what the circumstances of life may be. Faith is God's means of manifesting His glory through channels yielded to Him. In the words of the hymn, "Faith is the victory that *overcomes* the world," not *changes* the world so that it is easy to overcome.

Let's suppose you believe that God has perfect health for you, but in His providence you get sick. Now what do you do—especially as you see "Job's friends" approaching? How do you feel as they analyze the cause of your malady? How do you like being told that you've sinned? How do you go about trying to muster up more faith so that you can get well? How do you handle your guilt, your frustrations, your conflicts? What do you do when their theology doesn't work? Where do you turn for help? You really can't turn to your God, for He is a "God of health." What a terrible dilemma to be in! But quite a needless one really. The Bible warns, "Beware lest any man spoil you through philosophy and vain deceit, after the tradition of men, after the rudiments of the world, and not after Christ" (Col. 2:8). Be careful of a "health-and-wealth gospel" and a "God-exists-to-do-me-good philosophy." It could end in disappointment and consternation at the very time when you're crying for help.

Now, you may be thinking, "You've told me what *not* to say to someone passing through a crisis; could you please tell me what I *can* say?" That is an excellent question but one that stops me short. My mind races backwards to times when Lee and I have ridden quietly in hospital elevators, not really wanting to reach the right floor; to times when we have crossed the threshold of funeral homes and suddenly become paralyzed in speech. What *does* one say in times of crisis?

Perhaps it is better not to say anything at all! Job's friends were his greatest consolation during the days when they sat by his side saying nothing. The minute they started philosophizing about his condition, they began to hurt him. A kindness, a touch, a tear say more than volumes of well-planned speeches. God tells us to "weep with them that weep" (Rom. 12:15). Crying is not a sin. It can be a ministry. Our emotions are given to us by God to let others know we care. If we are required to speak, it is best to use God's words rather than our own. Not in a preachy way but with the full assurance that they "will not return void" (see Isa. 55:11) but will accomplish God's will for the moment.

13. Claiming God's Best

If God has a plan that is best for us, why then do we settle for second best? Why did the Israelites take 40 years to complete a journey that could have been made in 11 days? Why were they afraid to take the land that God had already given them? Why did they doubt God's promises and live in constant fear? Although there may be several legitimate answers to these questions, there is probably one answer that applies to all of them. The Israelites were simply willing to accept second best in their lives.

We usually think of "second best" as receiving less than God has in His bountiful plan. But I would like to suggest that receiving *more* than God wants to impart can also be considered "second best."

Now please understand the balance of truth. It is good for Christians to want everything that God has abundantly promised. The Bible says that as children of the King and joint-heirs with Christ, we have access to the riches of heaven. To not claim every blessing with our name on it is wrong in the eyes of God. To claim more than God has marked out for us, however, is equally wrong, I believe.

If "gimme, gimme, gimme" is the tone of our prayers, we're reaching too far into God's storehouse of blessings. There may be some things in His treasure chest that, if we receive them, will be used for personal glory instead of for the glory of God. There may be other things that, though good in themselves, will prove harmful if claimed at the wrong time. In His infinite wisdom God knows what things will bring Him glory and what things will benefit us the most. We do not. And yet sometimes we act as if we are the omniscient ones and He the finite servant, awaiting our bidding.

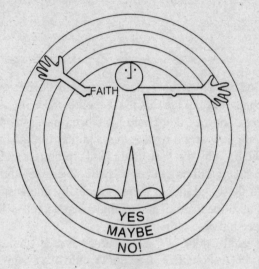

Figure 3

I think of every Christian as surrounded by three concentric circles (see fig. 3). His arm is the arm of faith reaching into the circles, sometimes farther than he should. The circle closest to him is marked ''yes.'' In it are blessings that are unquestionably in the plan of God—spiritual treasures such as eternal life, forgiveness of sins, freedom from guilt, peace that passes understanding, and conformity to the image of Christ. When we ask for these things, we don't have to attach the phrase ''if it be Thy will.'' We already *know* that it is His will because He says so in His Word. For example, if we confess our sins, forgiveness is ours. We receive it by faith, boldly making our claim because God has already assured us that He forgives all who confess their sins (see 1 John 1:9).

Difficulties come, however, when we try to reach beyond the "yes" circle into the "maybe" or the "no!" circles. Then our faith is no longer scriptural, it is presumptuous. Scriptural faith trusts God to do what *He* deems best. Presumptuous faith tempts God to do what *we* deem best. The latter often ends in heartbreak simply because what may seem to be a tremendous blessing at the time we are praying can turn out to be a terrible curse once we receive it.

In His sovereignty God sometimes grants us our desires but sends spiritual starvation to our souls. This is exactly what happened to the Israelites in the wilderness. They became tired of God's provision of manna and started clamoring for meat. And God, disgusted with their persistent nagging, decided, "All right! I'll give them meat!" And He did. So much meat that it saturated them to the point of nausea. And some even choked to death (see Num. 11:33).

God is ultimately wise in His decisions. And many earthly fathers have learned from His examples. When a child nags long enough and hard enough, Daddy may know of no better way of teaching him than by granting him his foolish desire and then letting him live with the consequences of his persistence. The Bible says God "gave them their request; but sent leanness into their soul" (Ps. 106:15). Christian, is that what *you* want? Your desires granted at the expense of your sanctification? Your petty will imposed upon His omniscient will?

How long is your arm of faith? Is it as long as that of George Müller, a giant of the faith, who trusted God for marvels that the rest of us can scarcely contemplate? Or is your arm short, quite within the realm of the ordinary? For Mr. Müller not to exercise the faith he had been given would be settling for a second best. This principle is as true for us as it was for him. But, realistically speaking, our arms may be shorter than Mr. Müller's. If this is the case, to stretch our faith to the proportions of his would be sheer presumption.

Man authors presumptuous faith; God authors scriptural faith. And the amount of faith He gives differs with the individual. He expects us to be good stewards, exercising every bit of faith that He has given us. Then He may give more. For those who are faithful with a little, He promises to make rulers over much (see Matt. 25:21). But He will not tolerate our reaching beyond the bounds that He has set for us.

It may help to remember that God is our King. He is royalty expressing itself, awesome to behold. At the time of the Hebrew sacrificial system, He was pictured as sitting upon His throne in His heavenly holy of holies, quite unapproachable except through a heavy veil. We praise His name that He tore that veil from top to bottom when His Son died for us upon the cross. And this Son Jesus Christ, risen with power over death, was the first person to enter God's presence without the intervention of a mediator. But even God's own Son approached the Sovereign delicately. "Not my will but thine be done" became His heavenly password. With those words He submitted Himself as a sacrifice, and His shed blood became the means by which the Son was granted full entrance into the Father's presence. Those were the words that caused the King to extend His scepter in favor toward His beloved Son. For His sovereignty was being acknowledged and His holiness duly honored.

Now we too are sons of God through the shed blood of Jesus Christ. Even so, dare we break the rules of kingly propriety that Christ Himself upheld so reverently? We should never forget that this great God whom we serve has the power to flick His finger and strike us dead, just as dead as Nadab and Abihu are because they entered God's presence their way (see Lev. 10:1,2). God said to Moses after their death, "I will be sanctified in them that come nigh me" (Lev. 10:3), and He meant it. Many years later when the disciples inquired of Christ the proper way to pray, He taught them to say, "Thy will be done" (Matt. 6:10). Are we so presumptuous as to think that we have found a better way to pray than the Father Himself espouses and His Son Jesus Christ teaches?

When we dictate to God to perform our bidding, He may not always act as forcefully with us as He did with Nadab and Abihu. In His grace, He may simply say no, and His refusal will stand no matter how bold we become. How many single men and women have insisted that God send them a mate, and God has simply said no? How many conscientious Christian businessmen and women have demanded promotion or wealth, and God has simply said no? How many suffering saints have claimed physical healing, and God has simply said no? If you have prayed in any of these ways—insisting, demanding, or claiming outside God's perfect will—you ought to be thankful that you are alive to relate your story. For God has been gracious to you.

If you know that you have been guilty of praying outside the will of God and God has definitely shown you your error by not granting your request, you might try examining the state of your heart while you were doing the praying. Was your faith lacking? Probably not. I am guessing that your faith may have been tremendous, but it was not scriptural faith. It was presumptuous faith. Now that you know the difference, perhaps you should ask God to teach you to pray *His* way.

The Bible states that faith substantiates God's plan for those of us who know Him (see Heb. 11:1). Without it, blessings remain in the realm of possibility. Through it, they become reality. The arm of faith grasps the blessings and brings them out of theory into experience. Claiming God's best requires that we emphasize in our lives the spiritual, not physical: "Seek ye first the kingdom of God, and his righteousness; and all these things shall be added unto you" (Matt. 6:33). God tells us, "Lay not up for yourselves treasures upon earth . . . But lay up for yourselves treasures in heaven" (Matt. 6:19,20). In other words, He wants our desires to be directed toward Him—not toward health, not toward companionship, not toward success—but toward Him. Then He will add to our treasury these other things according to what is best for us. And when we receive them, we will have the added blessing of knowing that they are in His perfect will.

The Lord says, "Present your bodies a living sacrifice, . . .that ye may prove what is that good, and acceptable, and perfect will of God" (Rom. 12:1,2). In other words, He wants our desires to be bound on the horns of the altar that *His* desires might be loosed in our lives. Letting our desires die may hurt, that's why it's called a sacrifice. But it is a *living* sacrifice. It won't kill us to make it. In fact, we will make it willingly if we truly want to give substance to the perfect will of God. Otherwise, our selfish desires will grow stronger and stronger. And we might even fall prey to assuming the precarious attitude that because we belong to God, God owes us something. Does He? No, God owes us absolutely nothing. In love He gives. But He knows nothing of owing. If you think so, you are thinking of yourself "more highly than [you] ought to think" (Rom 12:3). And that is presumption. God says, "Think soberly within the realm of faith that I have given you. That's how to prove My perfect will in your life."

What a restful way to live, trusting in the sovereignty of God! Gone is the pressure to muster up more faith. Gone is the burden of trying to figure out the most advantageous way to pray. Gone is the obligation to try to force God's hand. Instead there's sweet contentment, accompanied by freedom to praise my God "in whatsoever state I am" (Phil. 4:11). I thank the Lord that He knows what's best for me. And I claim every blessing that is marked with my name. If God wants to increase the length of my arm of faith, that would be exciting. But I'm not going to stretch it and lose my Christian balance. My greatest fear would be to receive the desire of my heart only to experience leanness in my soul.

14. Acknowledging His Sovereignty

If God is in control of all things, why doesn't He remove evil from our lives? It's a big question, one of the biggest that man ever asks, but it has an answer. God could remove evil if He wanted to, there is no question about that. In fact, He *will* remove it at some point in the future. Right now, though, He is making no effort to remove it because He has decreed to use it. It manifests His glory and, believe it or not, can actually benefit His children.

How can evil be used for good? In His awesome book of Ezekiel God shows us how. There He answers the question "Why?" and He does so 71 times. Interestingly, the answer is always stated in exactly the same way. Troubles happen in life, God says, "that ye may know that I am the Lord." Period. Does the answer seem too simple? It shouldn't. It is actually the core of the matter. To acknowledge the sovereignty of God is to fulfill one's purpose for living. To submit to a God who is in control of *all* of life brings tremendous peace to a Christian who has been sincerely examining pieces of a puzzle that don't seem to fit anywhere in the general scheme of things.

"That ye may know that I am the Lord." What does this phrase mean? Well, to me it means that when things go smoothly, I tend to get cocky. I feel in control, on top of life, like a master of my own destiny. But when tragedy strikes, especially tragedy upon tragedy, then suddenly I realize that I am *not* in control. God is in control. I have to acknowledge that He is the Lord.

In the book of Ezekiel God mentions many different situations in life, both good and bad—all of which He uses to get men to acknowledge His sovereignty. Let's examine several of these. Since we are dealing primarily with crises, let's select only difficult situations.

The first is a heartrending one: *tragic death*. Perhaps even now you are mourning a loved one, brutally torn from you by accident. Can any good at all come from such sorrow? God says yes. He may want to use your softness at this fragile time in your life to draw you closer to His bosom. Why don't you let Him do His perfect work? He says, "And the slain shall fall in the midst of you, and ye shall know that I am the Lord" (Ezek. 6:7).

Our next difficult situation involves *the wilderness experiences of life*—those times when we feel spiritually dry. God says, "So will I stretch out my hand upon them, and make the land desolate, yea, more desolate than the wilderness . . . and they shall know that I am the Lord" (Ezek. 6:14). God can use our deserts to cause spiritual thirst. And spiritual thirst leads to a satisfying drink from His living water. So next time you enter a desert, remember the water that waits in the oasis and take a long, cool drink.

Anyone who is concerned at all about the spiritual climate of our country agonizes over the present *decline in morals*. What does God have to say about nations that wander from His precepts? His words ring a solemn note: "The king shall mourn, and the prince shall be clothed with desolation, and the hands of the people of the land shall be troubled: I will do unto them after their way, and according to their deserts will I judge them; and they shall know that I am the Lord" (Ezek. 7:27).

National *destruction and desolation* are in God's hands. He adds, "And the cities that are inhabited shall be laid waste, and the land shall be desolate; and ye shall know that I am the Lord" (Ezek. 12:20). America, wake up and acknowledge the Lord in peace before you are forced to acknowledge Him in the devastation of judgment.

We Christians have become quite proficient in building walls of security around ourselves. Sometimes it takes troubles, *removal of security,* to show us that these are false walls, hastily built with shallow foundations. God says, "So will I break down the wall that ye have daubed with untempered morter, and bring it down to the ground, so that the foundation thereof shall be discovered, and it shall fall, and ye shall be consumed in the midst thereof: and ye shall know that I am the Lord" (Ezek. 13:14).

Have you ever been so beset by troubles that you feel as if you are jumping out of the frying pan into the fire, then out of the fire into a holocaust? Is God in control of such *multiplied disasters?* He claims to be. He says, "They shall go out from one fire, and another fire shall devour them; and ye shall know that I am the Lord" (Ezek. 15:7).

Or have you ever felt that life is really topsy-turvy with all sorts of things reversing direction? Do you know that God declares His sovereignty *in reversals* also: "And all the trees of the field shall know that I the Lord have brought down the high tree, have exalted the low tree, have dried up the green tree, and have made the dry tree to flourish: I the Lord have spoken and have done it" (Ezek. 17:24).

God moves sovereignly *in affliction*. He says, "As silver is melted in the midst of the furnace, so shall ye be melted in the midst thereof; and ye shall know that I [am] the Lord" (Ezek. 22:22). There is no question that the furnace is hot. But the purest gold comes from the hottest fire, especially when God is controlling the refining process.

God also moves sovereignly *in epidemics*. He says, "For

I will send into her pestilence, and blood into her streets; and the wounded shall be judged in the midst of her by the sword upon her on every side; and they shall know that I am the Lord" (Ezek. 28:23). Being part of a plague is a hard way to come to submission to the King of kings, but it is an effective way; for God determines life and death. Sometimes He makes that determination quite obvious.

Occasionally in God's dealings with men, He lets the *opposition* triumph. If you have ever had a dishonest businessman "do you in," you know what I mean. Why does God let honest citizens undergo abuse? Perhaps simply to reenforce His sovereignty. He says, "I will strengthen the arms of the king of Babylon, [the opposition], and the arms of Pharaoh shall fall down; and they shall know that I am the Lord, when I shall put my sword into the hand of the king of Babylon, and he shall stretch it out upon the land of Egypt" (Ezek. 30:25).

These are only 10 of God's repetitious statements. Read all 71 of them at one sitting and you will be overwhelmed by God's authority and power. How does one react to such total control of nature, of history, of men? I can answer only for myself. I am humbled. To me, disasters magnify God's sovereignty.

Not long ago a tornado swept through an area of homes not far from our house. I remember sitting on the living room floor with my children, shaking. Everybody was nervous, even the dog. None of us knew what to expect next. We watched the sky turn yellow, the wind begin to swirl in small black circles, and the lightning explode in balls of fire. We felt the thunder rend from us our complacency with life and our false sense of control.

As I sat there, small in the midst of God's greatness, I realized that I was quaking at His manifestation of power. Later, after the storm was past, several children in a friend's car pool were discussing the fury that they had just witnessed.

One speculated that God was angry. Another disagreed, then conceded, "Well, maybe a little."

The first child thought for a moment, then remarked, "What do you think it would be like if God *really* got mad?"

I appreciated hearing the account of this conversation, for I had been entertaining a similar question. I have known all along that God is sovereign, doing what He wants to do when He wants to do it, but every once in a while I need a fresh reminder. This particular one shaped me up for months to come.

God uses disasters to bring glory to Himself. He also uses them to benefit His children. But we cannot stop here, seeing God only in His fury; we must also see Him in His love. He promises that for those who trust Him, the curses of life will become blessings. With this realization, the sober book of Ezekiel starts to get exciting.

15. From Curse to Blessing

At one time or another we have all experienced how a curse has turned out to be a blessing in disguise. I was reminded of this truth one winter when our neighborhood was paralyzed by an ice storm. The emergency brought out the best in all of us. Neighbors whose greatest involvement before the storm was a casual wave on the way to work suddenly started sharing each other's generators, storing each other's food, and clearing each other's yards of debris. Not only did we get to know each other better, we had loads of fun in the process. Our crisis had become a real blessing.

Any crisis can become a blessing if you let it. But first you must be aware of God's complete control of every circumstance and His willingness to help you in your need. There are several ways that God deals with crises. Sometimes He actually prevents them from happening. This is a ministry of restraint which often goes unappreciated by us because we are not always aware of it. We may be delivered from evil several times in one day and not even know that God has intervened. Can you remember the last time you paused to thank God for what *could* have happened to you and didn't? Think of the accident that almost occurred on the freeway, the pencil point that just missed your child's eye as he fell, the storm that leveled the homes down the street but left yours intact. These are some of the more obvious times that God has intervened. There have been scores of other times when His hand of restraint was just as active; but for one reason or another you were oblivious to His care.

Another way that God deals with crises is to let them occur and *then* intervene on our behalf. When He moves in this way, He is fulfilling His promise in Ezekiel 34:25: "[I] will cause the evil beasts to cease out of the land." This type of deliverance is much more obvious to us than if God had stopped the "beast" before it attacked us. When we are in the jaws of a lion crying for help and then feel the lion go limp, our own mouths open in spontaneous praise; for we have tangible proof that God really cares for His own. But our proof is no more *real* than if God had restrained the crisis before it ever touched us.

As far as *real*, down-to-earth Christianity is concerned, I feel that perhaps God's most realistic ministry to us is His third way of dealing with crises. Sometimes He lets the crisis come, lets the crisis remain, but changes the curse of it to a blessing. In other words, He protects us not *from* the crisis but *in* the crisis, enveloping us with His bubble of love. It is obvious to all of us who have lived a while that God does not banish all difficult situations from our lives. There are many dry "wilderness" experiences to endure and the occasional frightening darkness of a "woods." But God promises that we will "dwell safely in the wilderness, and sleep in the woods" (Ezek. 34:25). In the midst of chaos, confusion, and despair, we can have peace that passes understanding in our souls. Whatever method God chooses for dealing with our crises—and *He* does the choosing, whether it be protection *from* our troubles or protection *in* our troubles—we have His assurance that He has chosen the right method for us. All He asks for is our trust.

Not only does God expect us to endure crises but actually to flourish through the adversity. This is where the book of Ezekiel becomes thrilling to read. God says, "The tree of the field shall yield her fruit" (Ezek. 34:27). According to Psalm 1:3, the tree of which God is speaking is one who trusts Him completely. Believers are trees "planted by the rivers of water," bringing forth fruit to His glory.

Perhaps Lee and I understand this figure of speech better than some people because we live in what used to be a pear orchard. On our property there are some two dozen pear trees, still actively bearing fruit. Often people stop and ask, "What kind of tree is that?" In the late summer, however, when the pears are starting to mature, nobody ever asks what kind of trees we have. They don't have to ask, all they have to do is look. The pears themselves are mute evidence of the nature of the trees which bear them. So it is with Christians. The fruit of our lives will manifest our nature. "By their fruits ye shall know them" (Matt. 7:20). The fruit of God's Spirit is love, joy, peace, longsuffering, gentleness, goodness, faith, meekness, and self-control (see Gal. 5:22,23), and is present in our lives for all the world to see.

As owners of pear trees, desiring a rich harvest, we treasure our pruning shears. They are our most important tool. We use them to cut out dead branches, to trim back live ones, and to control the general direction of our trees' growth. It is true that fewer pears result from this pruning. But the pears that do develop are better. They are heavy, succulent, and delicious—a real credit to their caretakers.

As the Caretaker of our lives, God prunes us. He wants bigger fruit to develop and flourish. Think a minute about yourself. If you were God, what method would *you* choose to produce bigger love in your life? Wouldn't it be to place quite near to you someone who is very hard to love? Where do you think bigger joy develops best? Isn't it right in the midst of despair? What's the most effective way to increase the growth of peace? Isn't it by introducing turmoil and trial? And how does longsuffering become mature? Isn't it through enduring pain and heartache? These are only four of God's "fruit of the

Spirit.'' If you do have any of them, how did they develop? If you answer that question objectively, you will probably have to admit that your times of greatest spiritual growth have been your times of greatest hardship.

Crises are God's pruning shears. They exist in the Christian's life to produce the fruit of His likeness. ''Every branch that beareth fruit, he [prunes] it, that it may bring forth more fruit'' (John 15:2). Love that abounds, joy that flourishes, peace that sustains, longsuffering that endures, and self-control that reigns—these are the evidence of a productive Christian life. Such evidence is not automatic but is the result of gentle pruning of a loving Caretaker.

With this realization, several questions arise in our minds. Does God have a right to prune His trees? I would think so. He made them, He owns them, and He wants them to produce abundantly. Does the pruning hurt the trees? Undoubtedly. When a branch that has been part of someone's life suddenly is no longer there, there is pain in that life. But only for a while. Healing begins immediately, touching more sore areas every day. And the vigor that is left in the life is directed into the branches that remain. The fruit that is produced through pruning is the most precious fruit of all.

I have often wondered how our pear trees feel when they see us approaching, shears in hand. Are they terrified? Helpless? Resigned? Perhaps all of these reactions are present. But when pear season comes, they are prosperous, fulfilling the purpose for which they were created.

Why are there crises in my life? In the Word of God lies a variety of answers. Perhaps the most significant answer to me personally is that crises accomplish the purpose for which I was made: to glorify God with my life. And they accomplish it more quickly and effectively than any other way I know.

When we personally bow to the sovereignty of God in our Christian growth, we bow to His right to do with us as He sees fit. We bow to His right to use pruning shears.

PART IV

WHAT DO CRISES ACCOMPLISH?

16. The Glory of Suffering

As we have seen in our study so far, the important question to ask is not, "Why are there crises in my life?" but rather, "What do life's crises accomplish?" Author Stuart Briscoe's answer to that question is, "Things happen *to* [me] in order that things should happen *in* [me] . . . so that things could happen *through* [me]."[3] A better answer will not be found.

Let me share with you the results of one of the most interesting discoveries that I have ever made while studying the Scriptures. It is the relationship between suffering and glory. Often the two ideas are linked, many times right in the same sentence. With this realization God's whole plan for man starts to unfold before us.

Remember the precious promises that we studied together in the book of Romans—promises made to those in the midst of life's crises? Let's go back there for a moment and pick up two verses that we overlooked before. As we read them, notice the connection between suffering and glory. Every time we come to one of those two words, I will *italicize* it for emphasis: "[We are] heirs of God, and joint-heirs with Christ; if so be that we *suffer* with him, that we may be also *glorified* together. For I reckon that the *sufferings* of this present time are not worthy to be compared with the *glory* which shall be revealed in us'' (Rom. 8:17,18).

A beautiful passage in 2 Corinthians expresses the same idea: ''For our light *affliction,* which is but for a moment, worketh for us a far more exceeding and eternal weight of *glory;* while we look not at the things which are seen, but at the things which are not seen: for the things which are seen are temporal; but the things which are not seen are eternal'' (4:17,18).

What does it mean to ''suffer with Christ''? How do life's sufferings ''work glory''? Turn to the book of 1 Peter to learn the answers to these questions. The theme of that book is suffering. Almost every time suffering is mentioned, ''glory'' follows in the same thought. The book begins with ''the *sufferings* of Christ, and the *glory* that should follow'' (1:11). Then it develops to include man and his troubles in life, especially the ''innocent'' member in the crises of relationships. God says, ''For this is thankworthy, if a man for conscience toward God endure grief, *suffering* wrongfully. For what *glory* is it, if, when ye be buffeted for your faults, ye shall take it patiently? but if, when ye do well, and *suffer* for it, ye take it patiently, this is acceptable with God'' (2:19,20).

The strongest passage regarding suffering occurs in the fourth chapter. Here we are told to expect afflictions in life because they are part of the human experience. God says, ''Beloved''—He is speaking to Christians—''Beloved, think it not strange concerning the fiery trial which is to try you, as though some strange thing happened unto you; but rejoice, inasmuch as ye are partakers of Christ's *sufferings;* that, when his *glory* shall be revealed, ye may be glad also with exceeding joy'' (4:12,13).

What does it mean to be ''partakers of Christ's sufferings''? Is this thought new to you? Perhaps you have always believed that suffering is satanic, that it is the devil's tool. Well, that thinking isn't entirely wrong; for suffering can very well be Satan's tool. But don't you know that Satan himself is

God's tool? And all of his devices, including suffering, can be used for the glory of God?

As we begin our Christian pilgrimage through life, bound for the state of eternal glory, God begins to mold us into the likeness of Himself. It is His desire (and should be ours) that by the time we reach the gate of heaven, there is not much left in us that has to be transformed. God accomplishes His sanctification in us by identifying us with His Son's experiences in life. We die with Christ; we are raised with Christ. We suffer with Christ; we are glorified with Christ. Our sufferings blend into His; His sufferings blend into ours. Our victory belongs to Him; His victory belongs to us. Paul says, "I am crucified with Christ; nevertheless I live; yet not I, but Christ liveth in me; and the life which I now live in the flesh I live by the faith of the Son of God, who loved me and gave himself for me" (Gal. 2:20).

In 1 Peter 4, we are admonished to remember our responsibility in suffering: it is that God may be glorified through our lives. Sometimes this goal is hard to reach, especially when we are being reproached. Even so, we are expected to do our part even though everyone else around us is mocking our testimony. God says, "If ye be reproached for the name of Christ, happy are ye; for the spirit of *glory* and of God resteth upon you; on their part he is evil spoken of, but on your part he is *glorified*" (4:14).

Verse 16 clearly establishes the fact that Christians suffer in life. In fact, God goes on to say in verse 19 that Christians suffer "according to the will of God." It shouldn't matter what the proponents of the "God-doesn't-want-anybody-to-suffer gospel" say to us. We who are looking at "things which are not seen" know that God will use our suffering as part of His plan for our lives. That plan ends in glory. God says, "If any man *suffer* as a Christian, let him not be ashamed; but let him *glorify* God on this behalf" (4:16).

Therefore, as crises arise, we should yield ourselves

afresh to our Maker. He is faithful to perform His promises in our lives. He says, "Let them that suffer according to the will of God commit the keeping of their souls to him in well doing, as unto a faithful Creator" (4:19).

The book ends with a benediction on sufferers: "But the God of all grace, who hath called us unto his eternal *glory* by Christ Jesus, after that ye have *suffered* a while, make you perfect, stablish, strengthen, settle you" (5:10). We learn in this verse that we are "called" unto suffering and glory—both. We also learn that suffering accomplishes four things in our lives: (1) it makes us perfect; (2) it establishes us; (3) it strengthens us; and (4) it settles us.

What is it that makes a suffering saint—one who in pain has yielded to God's purpose in his life—different from other people? The "yielded to God's purpose in his life" is an important part of the question, for some Christians become bitter through their experiences. But "yielding" produces a serenity, a "peace . . . which passeth all understanding" (Phil 4:7) in the life of the one who has surrendered. Every aspect of his being reflects it. His eyes invite friends to share. They are deep, placid, and victorious. His face, etched with trials and despair, comes alive as he shares the testimony that he has overcome tremendous obstacles. When he walks away, his steps are slow, deliberate, purposeful. The suffering saint has been "settled."

Sometimes when reading accounts of innocent prisoners facing death, I become impressed with the intensity of life that they seem to be experiencing. The importance of every moment is heightened as death awaits its prey. These accounts leave me feeling relieved, to be sure, that these trials have not been mine. Yet in a strange way I also feel left out. Please understand, it's not that I covet their pain. Indeed I abhor the injustice of man against man. But I do become aware that I am reading stories of individuals who are experiencing a fullness of life that very few people know.

Some words from the Gospel of John beg to be applied. Jesus said, "I am come that they might have life, and that they might have it more abundantly" (John 10:10). I ask myself, "What is God's 'abundant life'?" Is it quantity of years? No, it cannot be that. For some people "live" more in 30 years than others "live" in 60. Is it ease of life that Christ is talking about? No, it can't be that either. For His life could hardly be called easy. Yet He has called us to join Him in it. He said, "He that taketh not his cross, and followeth after me, is not worthy of me. He that findeth his life shall lose it; and he that loseth his life for my sake shall find it" (Matt. 10:38,39).

The "abundant life" is quality of living. It is intensity of purpose. It is yielding every moment to the glory of God, in the valleys of depression as well as on the peaks of elation. It is fullness of experience: suffering, tears, heartache, disappointment, failure, frustration and fear; along with happiness, laughter, rejoicing, victory, success, triumph, and glory. It is partaking of the gamut of emotions that Christ experienced for us.

When God calls us to the "abundant life," He calls us to all of it. He promises that "after we have suffered a while," He will make us perfect, establish, strengthen, and settle us. I particularly like the last verb. In a world that vacillates from one philosophy to another, it is a blessing from God to be "settled."

17. Rooted in Christ

Another way to describe being "settled" in faith is to speak of being rooted firmly in Christ. If you have ever enjoyed the shade of a mighty oak tree, you know the value of a good root system. Shallow roots produce weak trees. But deep roots produce strong trees. Since we all want to be as strong in our faith as possible, we need to find out how to send our roots down deep enough so that we are unshaken by life's storms.

Firm roots grow deep in search of water. Shallow roots, in contrast, are content to drink from the surface of the ground. If you are a shallow-rooted Christian, you can expect your crises to destroy you. If, on the other hand, you make a habit of drinking deeply from the living waters of God, you will become strong enough to go through the toughest crises that life may toss your way.

By definition, crises are life's turning points. They have the power to strengthen or to destroy. What the outcome is depends primarily on you and me—stay out of the Scriptures and fall flat, or get into the Word and grow strong.

In the fourth chapter of the Gospel of Mark, Christ shares

a pertinent parable. It is commonly called the parable of the sower. As you read it with me, ask yourself the following question: Which type of plant am I?

In the parable, we read how the seed of the Word of God falls upon four different types of lives and, consequently, produces four different results in those lives. Some seed falls on the wayside, where birds come and devour it. Christ explains that what happens in this case is that "Satan cometh immediately, and taketh away the word that was sown in their hearts" (Mark 4:15). It is a sad but inevitable result that wherever the Word of God is preached to a multitude of people, there are some who reject it.

Some seed falls on stony ground and springs up immediately in the shallow soil. But when the sun comes out, it withers because it has no root. There are some people "who, when they have heard the word, immediately receive it with gladness; and have no root in themselves, and so endure but for a time: afterward, when affliction or persecution ariseth for the word's sake, immediately they are offended" (4:16,17).

Some seed falls among thorns. It springs up only to be choked and ends up producing no fruit. Christ explains, "These are they which are sown among thorns; such as hear the word, and the cares of this world, and the deceitfulness of riches, and the lusts of other things entering in, choke the word, and it becometh unfruitful" (4:18,19).

The fourth plant is the only one that makes it through the crises of life. Its seed falls on good ground, yields fruit that increases, "some thirtyfold, some sixty, and some an hundred" (4:20). What we want to determine in this study is why the fourth plant survives and the others don't.

Our first clue lies in the nature of the seed. It is the productive Word of God. As you were reading Christ's explanation of the parable, did you notice how many times He mentioned His Word? Eight times! Why? Because without it there is no life. Without it there is no growth. And without it there is no victory.

For some reason, the typical Christian, upon finding himself enmeshed in a crisis, tends to neglect two of the most important aspects of his life: Christian fellowship and regular Bible reading. He may stop going to church altogether, and he may let his daily devotions wither to nothing. Either of these errors will eventually lead to problems but when coupled together, they breed disaster.

Daily feeding from the Word of God is an absolute necessity to enduring the crises of life. Whenever I am called upon to counsel a woman who is depressed, my first question is always, "Have you been in the Word of God today?"

Almost invariably the answer is no. I have come to expect that answer. For if the depressed woman had been in the Word that day, there is a good possibility that she would not have had to call me. God would have been her present help in trouble. I am not saying that just reading the Word of God will overcome all the depressing situations in life. I know better than that. But I am saying that we tend to ignore our closest and greatest help in trouble: the pertinent Word of God.

There seems to be a direct correlation between the amount of Scripture in a life and the amount of victory in that same life—little Bible study, little victory; great amounts of Bible study, great victory. There is only one thing more important than the written Word of God. And that is the living Word of God, the Lord Jesus Christ.

The seed of the Word, however, must fall on good ground in order to produce lasting results. A seed which opens in fertile soil sends down a root. The more the soil is watered, the deeper the root goes. It is the root that gives the plant stability. It is also the root that enables the plant to produce fruit. Without a root the plant will not survive. Without fruit the plant might as well not exist at all.

Look at figure 4, which illustrates the four types of life

situations represented in the parable, and try to answer the question, Which of the four represent true Christians?

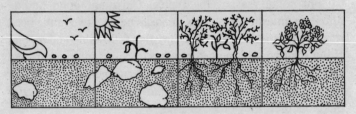

Figure 4

We probably all agree that situation number 1 depicts unquestionably a nonbeliever simply because nothing at all happens when the seed of the Word of God touches his life. So we will leave him in his doom for the moment.

Now skip over to number 4. His status is obvious also. He is a real, honest-to-goodness Christian, blossoming for God. His seed was broken before Satan had a chance to snatch it. His roots are deep, giving him stability. And he is producing an abundance of fruit.

The problem comes with the persons in numbers 2 and 3. Both these plants exhibit life, at least for a while. At first glance they look as if they might amount to something. But at second glance we notice that they have no roots. If there are no roots, there will be no fruit. And fruit is our measuring stick. The Bible says, "By their fruits ye shall know them" (Matt. 7:20). So we are forced to conclude that plants 2 and 3 are professing Christians only. There is no evidence other than what they say that they are rooted in Christ.

If the seed is the Word and the roots are the stability resulting from the opening of the Word, what is the fruit? Some Christians are under the impression that fruit is religious activity. They keep running from one involvement to another, doing much but accomplishing little.

Others think that fruit is people they have personally

"converted" to Christ. Their self-imposed (and sometimes others-imposed) pressure for "decisions" creates in them an unnatural responsibility and increasing frustration. They spend their Christian lives carrying terrible burdens of guilt because they have not won enough souls to Christ. This guilt tends to make them ineffective at the very time when they wish to be most effective: when they are faced with the opportunity to share the claims of Christ with a truly hungry soul.

Although both involvement and soul-winning are vital parts of the Christian experience, they are not the essence of "fruit." For it is possible for non-Christians to be totally involved in their churches, doing the Lord's work in the efforts of the flesh. It is even possible for non-Christians to be used by the Lord in a soul's conversion.

What? Is such a statement not blasphemous? No. If you diligently search the Scriptures dealing with evangelism, you should come to the conclusion that souls are saved by God, not by men. Furthermore, the Lord employs His Word rather than man's arguments to make man's spirit receptive. The Bible says, "Faith cometh by hearing, and hearing by the word of God" (Rom. 10:17). In other words, if the Word of God is employed, God will honor it regardless of the nature of the vessel through which it comes. In this crazy world of ours where many unusual things happen, genuine conversions have been known to result through the preaching of flagrantly offensive "evangelists."

In the Word of God lies glorious freedom for anyone who is bound by the shackles of having to do "more" for God. It is freedom from "doing" to freedom of "being." When we understand that God is more interested in our nature than in our activity, we are released to serve Him effectively. And when we understand where our responsibility starts and stops, we are released to become effective witnesses. There is clearly a division of labor in witnessing—it is *our* responsibility to present the claims of Christ, it is *God's* responsibility to save the soul.

If, then, the primary fruit of the Christian life is neither activity nor number of converts, what is it? *It is the likeness of the Son of God.* Christlikeness. The Lord puts it this way, "The fruit of the Spirit is love, joy, peace, longsuffering, gentleness, goodness, faith, meekness, and self-control" (Gal. 5:22,23). Active Christian involvement and soul-winning are indeed part of this fruit. But they are natural results of a life that is God-centered rather than the essence of the Christian life itself. In other words, God is more interested in what we *are* than in what we do. If we *are* what we should be, it automatically follows that we will be doing what we should be doing. It is *our* responsibility to yield ourselves to God's control. It is *God's* responsibility to use our yielding to bless the lives of others.

If we truly want the fruit of God's Spirit to be manifested in our lives, our primary concern should be to open the seed of the Word of God each day. This seed will send down roots which, in turn, will stabilize our growth so that we can endure the crises that appear above the ground. There is no other way to make it through life's vale of tears than to be firmly rooted in Christ through His Word.

18. Nothing but Leaves

All plants are not firmly rooted and the anticipated fruit never comes. We once had such a plant in our garden. In fact, it was Greg who planted the seed and proudly proclaimed to the family that this year *he* would supply our pumpkins for Halloween.

Daily Greg ran to the garden. And daily he gave us his progress report. One day he announced a green shoot. Another day, a vine that had grown a foot overnight. In a month there was a proliferation of leaves. Indeed, it was the healthiest pumpkin plant we had ever seen.

Gradually, however, Greg was starting to become uneasy. So were the rest of us. Where were the little nodules that would eventually become our pumpkins? We looked under every leaf, but our search proved to be in vain. Would we have pumpkins by the end of October?

We never did. The plant went on to take over the whole garden. It grew and it grew and it grew. But it produced not even one pumpkin. All its efforts went into its leaves. "What a waste!" our family sighed, disappointment showing on our faces. Then we went out and bought our Halloween pumpkins. As we handled the plump orange fruit, we concluded that the farmer that supplied us must have had plants with fewer leaves than ours had.

Jesus Christ had a similar experience. During the week of His passion, He approached a fig tree and saw "nothing but leaves" (Mark 11:13). Since He was looking for fruit, He cursed the tree. This tree received only one chance to prove its nature to God. In a parable Jesus taught, another more fortunate tree received a second chance. As God's sword of judgment was about to cut it to the ground, a mediator interceded, "Lord, let it alone this year also, till I shall dig about it, and dung it: and if it bear fruit, well: and if not, then after that thou shalt cut it down" (Luke 13:8,9). Some people receive more time than others to prove the nature of their faith. Regardless of the amount of time granted, however, both scriptural accounts prove one fact: God is looking for the fruit of His Spirit. Without that, there is no evidence whatsoever that the Spirit of Christ dwells within.

As we have seen in our study of the parable of the sower, the plants in pictures 2 and 3 both look like Christians—both appear to have life; both endure for a time. But they have no roots in the Word of God. Therefore, they produce no fruit of the Spirit. A disturbing question arises in our minds: If they have no root, how can they grow at all?

The answer lies in understanding that there are four different types of faith: historical, miraculous, temporary, and saving. Historical faith is an intellectual faith. The one who possesses it believes that Jesus Christ was a historical figure who lived, died, was buried, and rose from the dead. All of this vital information is stored in his head. But the head knowledge never finds its way to his heart. He will not trust Christ for his salvation.

Miraculous faith trusts God to do the supernatural. The one who has it may ask for healing and truly believe that God can perform it. In His sovereignty God may answer the prayer. But the man with this type of faith wants only the miracle. He doesn't want the Lord. Belief in a God of miracles also accompanies saving faith; but the frightening realization is that this belief can exist by itself. It accounts for miracles in the lives of non-Christians. It also accounts for the piles of crutches that cured folks leave at shrines—shrines that sometimes exalt human beings over the Lord Himself.

Temporary faith is the most interesting of the false faiths. It exists quite sincerely—for a while. People confronted with harrowing "lifeboat-type" experiences have been known to exercise this type of faith. They entrust their lives to God—for as long as they are in the lifeboat. But shortly after they are back on land, they seem to want little to do with their Saviour. He demands control of their lives *all* of the time. And total control is one thing that they do not want to relinquish.

The most deceiving characteristic of temporary faith is that it looks exactly like the beginnings of saving faith. Only one thing proves which is which: time. If the fig tree does not bear figs in a given amount of time, it is cut down. If a professing Christian does not produce evidence of his new birth in a given amount of time, he too will be "cut down." His faith has endured only temporarily.

Saving faith has two intrinsic qualities that the other three types of faith are lacking: it is persevering, and it is fruit-producing. The Bible says, "He that endureth to the end shall be saved" (Matt. 10:22). The context in which this passage is written is crisis-filled. Christ says to His disciples, "I send you forth as sheep in the midst of wolves: . . . beware of men . . . they will scourge you . . . ye shall be brought before governors and kings for my sake, . . . the brother shall deliver up the brother to death, and the father, the child: and the children shall rise up against their parents, and cause them to be put to death" (Matt. 10:16-21). How's that for a series of crises? Yet in all these troubles the saving faith endures.

Not only does it endure, it actually grows stronger. Christ promises, "Your sorrow shall be turned into joy. . . . In the world ye shall have tribulation; but be of good cheer; I have overcome the world" (John 16:20,33).

Another question arises, naturally, at this point. Do we have a right to judge another person's spiritual condition? Referring to the illustration of the seed, we notice that we finite beings cannot see below the ground. We don't know if there is a root to the plant or not. Only God knows that. But we certainly can see above the ground. We can see if there is fruit. In the life of any Christian, genuinely dedicated to bringing God glory, there *should* be enough fruit present to make his salvation obvious.

A Scripture passage that is often quoted out of context is the first verse of the seventh chapter of Matthew. It reads, "Judge not, that ye be not judged." How many times is it quoted in a lifetime to cover all kinds of situations? Actually, it is not a universal statement; it was never meant to apply to every situation. In fact, Christ goes on to mention two situations in which it must not apply. The first occurs in verse 6. He says, "Give not that which is holy unto the dogs, neither cast ye your pearls before swine, lest they trample them under their feet, and turn again and rend you." In order to distinguish a pig from a sheep, we have to make a judgment. Otherwise, we may be spiritually torn to pieces.

The second situation occurs in verse 15: "Beware of false prophets, which come to you in sheep's clothing, but inwardly they are ravening wolves." How do we tell a false prophet without making a judgment?

The answer is we can't.

As plants struggling to survive in tangled gardens, we Christians are under no obligation to judge those plants with which we are not directly involved, but look as if they might be a threat to us. It is engrossing enough to worry about our own problems without worrying about God's too. The Lord has all deceivers under His control. He says that He intends to let the tares grow with the wheat until the harvest. Then He, not we, will remove the tares and burn them. If we try to do God's weeding for Him, we might injure some of His precious plants. So it is best to leave the plants which are "on the other side of the fence" alone.

Our real problems are not with the distant plants anyway, but with the nearby ones that want to entwine themselves around our lives. When this happens, we had better make a judgment about their spiritual condition fast, for our own spiritual stability is being threatened. If we are not discerning, we run the risk of being trapped by any cultist who happens to knock on our door. And there seems to be an endless variety of them today, aggressively trying to ensnare Christians.

The most frightening part of this chapter we are studying begins in verse 21. Here we meet people who from most outward appearances belong to the family of God. Their profession of Christ is proper. They openly call Him "Lord." But God says, "Not every one that saith unto me, Lord, Lord shall enter the kingdom of heaven."

These religious worshipers even prophesy in the name of Christ and in His name cast out demons. Let's stop here for a moment while the thrust of this activity sinks in. Let's imagine ourselves in the midst of a spectacular miracle service: the name of Christ is being spoken; entranced folks are "prophesying" with beautiful language; the oppressed are being freed from demons; people charged with emotion are testifying that they have been healed. But we are uneasy. Why? Is it possible that this type of service may not be of God?

It is indeed possible. Christ says that many will say to Him in the day of judgment, "Lord, Lord, have we not prophesied in thy name? and in thy name have cast out devils?" And then He will say unto them, "I never knew you: depart from me, ye that work iniquity" (7:22,23).

Now remember, these prophets are performing their miracles in the name of Christ! That startling fact is emphasized three times in one verse. And they have great power, power over the kingdom of darkness itself. If these miracle-workers are not true Christians, then where in the world is their tremendous power coming from? There are three possible answers I think.

The first possible source is *the Lord Himself*. He is not limited to working through holy individuals. In our examination of miraculous activity, we must never lose sight of the fact that God Himself is the one who performs miracles. He is the source of true supernatural activity. There has to be an original Creator in order for there to be copies of His work. And this Creator is just as capable of performing miracles today as He was in the days of old. When we find ourselves confronting the supernatural, our first thoughts should be toward God. If He is truly performing the miracle in question, His Spirit will bear witness with ours that He is in our midst. If we experience unrest, we should examine some other possibilities for the seemingly supernatural activity.

Another possible source of power is the *power of Satan*. In the past, he has shown the ability to counterfeit some of the miracles of God. When Moses used the rod of God's judgment against the Egyptians, the sorcerers "also did in like manner with their enchantments" (Exod. 7:11). As we study the Scriptures, we learn that this type of counterfeit activity will increase as the end of the age draws nigh. There will be much "working of Satan with all power and signs and lying wonders" (2 Thess. 2:9). Notice that the wonders will "lie." They will appear to be from God when, in fact, they are from Satan. I feel that Christians today need the gift of discernment as they have never needed it before.

Still another possibility, some suggest that "miracles" or the appearance of miracles can be *psychologically induced* by man. Under great emotion and stress, men can cause themselves to "prophesy." They can also will themselves well from certain sicknesses. Even if we go no further in our study of such activities than we have already gone, we have enough alternatives as to the source of miracle-working power to keep us from automatically assuming that everything that smacks of the supernatural is of God. It is not.

These "false prophets" who say the right words and dazzle people with their miracles have one other impressive credential: they do "many wonderful works." Again their performance is in the name of Christ. They give to the poor, they fight for justice, they help the oppressed, and they meet their neighbors' needs. In the area of social involvement, counterfeit Christians often put genuine Christians to shame.

With so many spectacular activities punctuating the Christian scene today, is there any way to de-mask the false prophet? Yes, there is. Whenever in doubt, ask life's most discerning question: Is this activity to the glory of God or to the glory of man? Who is lifted up in exaltation, the miracle-worker or the Lord? Then call for a showing of the performer's fruit. The Bible says that though he speaks "with the tongues of men and of angels, and has not love, he is become as sounding brass or a tinkling cymbal. And though he has the gift of prophecy and understands all mysteries and all knowledge; and though he has all faith, so that he could remove mountains, and has not love, he is nothing. And though he bestows all his goods to feed the poor, and though he gives his body to be burned, and has not love, it profits him nothing" (see 1 Cor. 13:1-3).

As it is with love, so it is with the rest of the fruit of the Spirit of God—with joy, peace, longsuffering, gentleness, goodness, faith, meekness and self-control. These are the marks of a Christian. God says, "By their fruits ye shall know them" (See Matt. 7:16). Activity doesn't count. Miracles don't count. Public profession doesn't count. Converts don't count. And good works don't count. They are all nothing but leaves. Only one thing counts in discerning a Christian from a non-Christian: the fruit of his life before God and man.

19. The Believer's Choice

No sooner had I returned from speaking at a retreat in one of our southern states, than I received a letter from a woman with whom I had been counseling. She explained that although she had been active in church work for many years, she had really been doing the Lord's work in the efforts of the flesh. While studying with me the seventh chapter of the Gospel of Matthew, she was confronted with the emptiness of her activity for God, and she was miraculously saved. Her letter states, "II Corinthians 5:17 says, 'Therefore, if any man be in Christ Jesus, he is a new creature; old things are passed away; behold, all things are become new.' I am a new creature! I have a new life. For the first time in my life I consider myself 'dead to sin but alive to God in Christ Jesus.' My alcohol problem is gone, my sex problem is gone, and my independence appears to be gone. Oh, I'm not saying that there's nothing left for God to do. Everyday He shows me another room to start housecleaning. Matthew 7:20-23 were the verses that God used to take the patches off my eyes. Then I realized that I did not have the fruit of the Spirit manifested in my life. Today, I can see this fruit with blooms!"

Isn't that an exciting letter? The same new life that this woman is experiencing is available to all who place their trust in Christ.

Let's look again at the illustration of the sower. We want to determine why two of the plants don't make it through the hard times of life. They endure "but for a time," then crises kill them. Come, if you will, through a series of mental gymnastics with me.

What causes plant number 2 to wither?

"The sun."

What does the sun represent?

"Affliction and persecution."

Why are affliction and persecution able to harm the plant?

"Because it has no root."

True. The so-called believer represented by plant number 2 has been taught that affliction and persecution are not part of God's plan for His children. He has not studied for himself the subject of suffering and pain. Therefore, when suffering appears, he is at a loss. "Hey, this wasn't part of the package!" he exclaims and walks away from God—the God of his imagination.

He bears no fruit because he has no root. He has no root because his seed was not properly broken. The application is strong. Our study of the Word of God establishes our foundations. The more we assimilate it, the deeper our foundations go. Then when the crises of life do come, we cannot be moved. For we have come to realize that we are being privileged to partake of Christ's sufferings. And that theology produces tremendous, sustaining power.

Let me pose a second round of questions.

What causes plant number 3 to be choked?

"Thorns."

What do the thorns represent?

"The cares of this world, and the deceitfulness of riches, and the lusts of other things" (Mark 4:19).

Why are the thorns able to kill the plant?

"Because it has no root."

Look at plant number 4 again. *Are there any birds in the air over this plant?*

"No. There aren't any birds in the drawing."

Let me rephrase the question. *Should I add birds in the air over the fourth plant?*

"Yes!"

Why?

"Because there is great satanic activity surrounding the life of a Christian."

Indeed there is. In fact, there may be more satanic activity surrounding the life of a Christian than there is surrounding the life of a non-Christian. After all, Satan already owns the non-Christian. He used to own the Christian too but lost him to another Master at the moment of the Christian's adoption into the family of God. Now Satan desperately wants him back. But he can't get to a seed that has already been broken. He can't get to roots that have tunneled into the soil. The Word of God protects the Christian and frustrates his enemy. I will add birds to the fourth picture. Lots of them.

Another question. *Is there a sun over plant number 4?*

"There should be."

Why?

"Because plants can't grow without sun."

Right. Affliction and persecution are part of the Christian life. But rather than causing this plant to wither, they strengthen it instead. The sun—affliction and persecution—is necessary for healthy growth. I will draw one next to the birds in the fourth picture.

One more question. *Are there any thorns in the garden of plant number 4?*

Now you know what I'm getting at, don't you? Of course there are thorns in the garden. Whose life doesn't have cares? But rather than choking the life from the fourth plant, they cause it to fight and grow stronger each day. Now, plant number 4 looks like figure 5.

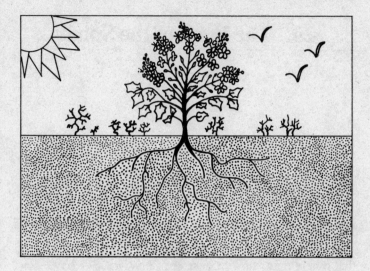

Figure 5

Thus a thrilling truth unfolds. The influences that cause the rootless plants to die are the very same influences that cause the plants with roots to grow. They provide nourishment, they develop perseverance, and they establish priorities in life. When a life is committed to God, curses are turned to blessings.

The past persecution of the Christian church has strengthened its impact on the world. The future persecution of the same church will separate the nominal believers from those truly committed to Christ. Crises make the difference. They destroy or they strengthen. The choice of outcome lies with you. Will you embrace a shallow theology based on your own desires? Or will you be diligent to break the seed, send down roots, and let the power of God surge through you? The choice you make will determine the direction of the rest of your life. Make it wisely, prayerfully, and in the fear of God.

20. The Fruit of the Spirit

We have talked about the necessity of producing fruit so that others may know that we are Christians. We have seen two plants that produced nothing and one plant that produced in abundance. The last plant was the one Jesus approved.

Now at this point I imagine that some of you may be feeling a little uneasy. In the light of the illustration of the different types of plants, you have honestly examined your own life and have found it sorely lacking. You are certain that you have saving faith, but you wonder about the fruit of the Spirit.

So that there will arise in the hearts of you new believers no uncertainty concerning your precious salvation, I want to point out that there is a time at which plant number 4 looks exactly like 2 and 3. Its beginnings are small. And when it begins to produce fruit, it may not come in great quantities. The Bible says that some produce thirty-fold; some, sixty-fold; and some a hundred-fold. But they *all* produce fruit.

The late George Slavin, former pastor of the Highland Park Baptist Church in Southfield, Michigan, used to liken saving faith to a tiny black watermelon seed. He would challenge his congregation in the following way: ''Suppose for a moment that you have never seen a watermelon. Have you got that? You have never seen a watermelon. Someone comes up to you and shows you a flat black seed. Then he tells you that if you plant the seed in good soil, water it properly, and expose it to the sun, it will quickly grow into a long, twining vine. Eventually a large green melon will appear, over a foot long. It will have stripes on the outside and an inch-thick white rind around the edge. The inside of the melon will be the most luscious, red, thirst-quenching delight that you have ever tasted. And the whole inside will be dotted with flat black seeds, just like the one you planted weeks ago.

"Now if you have never seen a watermelon," Rev. Slavin would continue, "and I tell you a story like that, you will probably say, 'Come on. You're kidding me. All *that* from a little black seed?' "

Yes, all *that* from a little black seed—and the power of God. So it is with faith. All we need is a little. But a little of the right kind—faith that endures, faith with the potential for fruit, true saving faith. The type of faith that under God's care flourishes into something stupendous: big succulent love, large abounding joy, peace that expands in crises. Day by day its fruit grows and delights us. It is marvelous to behold!

The fruit of the Spirit matures in the sun, thrives among thorns, and defies the attacks of birds. God's love grows best when challenged; God's joy begins to flourish in the midst of tribulation; God's peace is produced through turmoil; long-suffering comes through pain; gentleness, through abrasion; goodness, through evil bombardment; faith, through struggles with doubt; meekness, through battles with pride; self-control, through tense situations. These qualities are primary fruit. God expects them first in a life.

Let me go once more to our illustration and draw a pear on the ground underneath plant number 4. This pear is secondary fruit. When love grows so big that it drops, it starts another plant. When joy gets so big that *it* drops, then *it* starts another plant. And so the fruit multiplies. In other words, our responsibility in life is to emulate the character of Christ. His responsibility through us is to add precious souls to His kingdom.

This concept of witnessing naturally should relieve pressure and guilt from you Christians who are already too uptight about what you are *not* doing for God. It should free you to carry out your own responsibility and let God carry out His. When we stand before our Saviour in judgment, He will not ask, "How many scalps have you got on your belt?" Instead, the question will be, "How have you glorified me with your life?"

Peter says, "But the God of all grace, who hath called us unto his eternal glory by Christ Jesus, *after that ye have suffered a while,* make you perfect, stablish, strengthen, and settle you. To Him be glory and dominion forever and ever. Amen." (1 Pet. 5:10,11, italics added).

I think of each one of us as a flower, fashioned by God Himself. We differ in variety, in color, and in shape. Yet each one of us is uniquely beautiful to our great Creator. Although we all live in separate gardens, our problems are quite the same. Weeds, thorns, and briers abound, making us struggle to survive. We cry to our Lord for help.

As the loving Gardener looks down from above, He thoroughly understands our needs. He speaks to us with love. "Precious flower," He says, "I hear your cry. I see your plight. I love you. As caretaker of your life, I have three options open to me. I could pluck you out of your turmoil and woe and place you in a vase in my heavenly mansion. You would be very beautiful there. When I do pluck my flowers, sometimes I choose buds, fresh in their delicacy, ready to burst into bloom. Other times I choose full flowers, developed to capacity, gorgeous to behold. I could pluck you too. But I have decided not to. At least not yet.

"Or, I could rototill the weeds from your garden. Then you would have no struggle—no struggle and no testimony.

You would be left alone, weak, without appreciation whatsoever for my sustaining power in trials. So, I'm not going to do that either.

"I'm going to take the third option. I will leave you in your garden, right in your tangled mess. I will leave you with a message rather than a miracle: Lift your face to the sun. Catch my droplets of refreshment. Let them bathe your petals and leaves, enriching your soil with their minerals. Send your roots down deep, then wait for me to surge through you with power. I will strengthen you by my might in the inner man 'that ye might be filled with all the fulness of God' (Eph. 3:19), be a manifestation of my glory in a world that needs to see beauty. In other words, dear flower, 'Bloom where you are planted.' "

One evening as Lee and I were sharing this particular analogy of the flowers, one lady, obviously still quite distressed in her crisis, asked me when the course was going to turn from the negative to the positive. I told her I hoped that this would be the night. As I finished the presentations of God's options, I stole a look at her face. Her eyes were brimming with tears. In my heart I silently prayed that her spiritual turning point would come. Then I added a prayer that the final portion of our course on crises would escalate to victory.

PART V

HOW CAN I HAVE VICTORY?

21. Emotion or Action?

My husband Lee loves to go jogging. If you were to watch him don his sweat suit, put on his florescent running shoes, and adjust his headband over his ears, you would know immediately that he is a born runner. He looks like one. That's all there is to it.

I sometimes go jogging too. Not because I enjoy it and not because I am good at it. I go just because Lee likes company. Actually, the company is rather limited because I can hardly make it to the end of the street. There the two of us part. While Lee goes on to complete his five-mile exercise, I come home and flop on the floor.

Because of this frustrating experience which repeats itself regularly, I have concluded that God makes joggers and non-joggers. I am a non-jogger. I will never be anything else. Every step is painful for me. Now Lee experiences pain too, he admits, but somehow he is able to get past the hurting into a state of euphoria. "Sometimes I feel as if I could run all night," he says. I can only imagine what such exhilaration must be like.

Life is a lot like jogging. The painful times are the crises and the post-pain euphoria, the victory. There is one big difference, however, between running the streets of a neighborhood and running the race of life. In life, every Christian is a jogger. He has a built-in motivation for getting past the pain. You see, he *knows* that God can make him a winner. Such assurance should build tremendous confidence.

The trouble is it doesn't always do so. What we know in our heads is hard to put into practice in our lives. We need some practical coaching on running, some understanding of the role that discipline, perseverance, and endurance play. You see, runners don't just quit because they feel like quitting. If feelings determined their actions, they would never run at all. Good feelings don't come until after the pain. Yet many of us try to run life's race controlled completely by feelings. The result can be disastrous. Let me show you what I mean.

A personal pattern of defeat might progress like this: A crisis enters my life, so I start feeling sorry for myself. Then I become depressed *because* I have been feeling sorry for myself. Then when I realize how depressed I am, I begin to feel even *more* sorry for myself. If this oppressive pattern continues to dominate me, I may become desperate enough to take my own life. When one is at the bottom of the pit of depression, suicide sometimes presents itself as the only escape from a very negative life-style.

The person reasoning in such a way is controlled by his feelings. Each emotion he has leads progressively to a deeper one, the end of which precipitates negative action. A life that was created to bring glory to God sadly ends in defeat. Instead of glorifying God, the victim of depression glorifies himself. It is himself he pities. It is himself he serves. And it is himself he catapults into eternity. Negative feelings send a person spiraling downward at a terrifying pace. If those feelings are not reversed, they will obliterate the life they've mastered. Diagramed, the situation looks like figure 6.

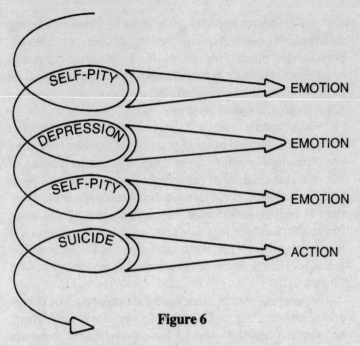

Figure 6

Fortunately, the downward spiral can be reversed at any point short of suicide. But I must take several actions to reverse it.

I must realize first that self is not the essence of life. God is. He made me for His glory. And He made me just as I am. So, a point at which the spiral may begin to reverse itself is *the point at which I accept myself.* Whatever flaws and shortcomings I possess, God controls. The Bible says, He "covered me in my mother's womb" (Ps. 139:13). Now that I have committed my life to Him in saving faith, I belong to Him as part of His family. He accepts me in His beloved Son (see Eph. 1:6). If I can be accepted—just as I am—by the Holy God of the universe, it stands to reason that I should be able to accept myself. Then the spiral of my life will begin to point upward.

A second point at which the spiral can be reversed is *the*

point at which I accept my crisis. Not only must I accept myself as I am, I must also accept my life as it is. Some Christians go through their whole earthly pilgrimage fighting the sovereignty of God. I know. I've met lots of them. In fact, I've spent some time in that state myself. The end is unrest, conflict and perpetual frustration.

But I've learned that I don't have to be so miserable. I can submit to the sovereignty of God in my life and be at peace with myself, at peace with my circumstances, and at peace with my Lord. But the choice is up to me. Whether I acknowledge the fact or not, God *is* in control of my life. So, why not acknowledge it and submit to it and enjoy the victory that follows?

A third injunction in reversing the spiral is *to exercise self-discipline*. Now that I have determined to be controlled by my will instead of by my feelings, I must use that will to obey my Lord's commandments. What He tells me to do I must do, whether I feel like doing it or not. When His spiritual alarm goes off, I am to jump out of bed immediately. If I start thinking about whether I feel like getting up or not, I may end up in bed the rest of the day. When God gives a command in His Word, He doesn't expect me to analyze it, test it, think about it, and see if I feel like doing it. He expects me to obey. Obedience leads to victory.

A fourth command that has power to reverse the downward spiral is *to be involved in the lives of others*. When I reach out in love, it automatically follows that I will come face to face with the burdens other people carry—huge burdens, burdens that make my own problems shrink in comparison. This therapy rarely fails. In fact, in helping to lighten someone else's load, I may forget my own difficulties altogether. In giving, I will gain. Victory will be mine. It is a scriptural principle that has been proven time and time again. Now I need to prove it in my own life.

Diagramed, the reversed spiral looks like figure 7.

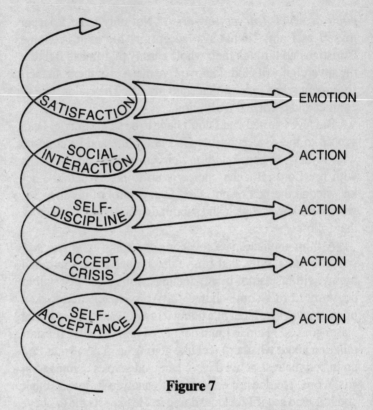

Figure 7

Obedience to God's positive instruction produces an amazing corollary: positive feelings follow. Someone has wisely said, "Act the way you want to become, and you will become the way you act." Becoming the person God wants me to be affects all aspects of my being, including my emotions. In fulfilling God's purpose for my life, I not only *do* good. I also *feel* good. I am living to the glory of God. I *know* I am living to the glory of God. And because I *know* it, I have His precious victory.

22. A Widow's Victory

So far in our study of victory, we have seen that what we do about our crises is a big factor in determining whether we come out winners or losers. If we make up our minds to be winners, we will surely enjoy success. If, on the other hand, we give in to an attitude of failure, we will lose the battle every time.

I would like to share with you an example of someone who is an overcomer. I am selecting this particular person for my illustration because I have been privileged to watch her reactions for long enough to proclaim her a winner. I lived with her before her crisis occurred and observed her contentment with life. Then I visited her after tragedy struck and watched her put God's principles into action. Today I see her coping nicely with the challenges that advancing years are bringing. I have chosen to share her story because I know it. I am also sharing it because I love the one who is making that story happen. She is my beloved mother.

Mother's crisis was the loss of her husband, my father, leaving her a widow in the prime of life. Just when our family's financial obligations were almost all met and Mom and Dad could really begin to enjoy life together, there was suddenly no life together to enjoy. Death entered and shattered a marriage. It shattered a family as well.

Daddy's death was not entirely unexpected. He had had a history of heart trouble and a couple of really close calls. But the date God chose to take him home seemed to us to occur at a terribly inconvenient time. I guess when I think about it, though, there is really no convenient time to die.

We had recently celebrated Christmas with a family reunion. As Lee and I drove up the snow-covered lane to the New Jersey farmhouse, we remarked how beautiful the old homestead looked snuggled in its blanket of white. Everybody was there to meet us: Daddy in his deer-hunter's shirt, Mother in her apron, my sister Polly and her husband with their two active preschoolers, and my teenage sister Diane. Since we saw each other infrequently because of the distance involved, our greetings were long and meaningful. Christmas was the one event of the year that every member of the family made a special effort to attend. I watched Daddy lean down and whisper a promise in the ears of our toddler Dirk. By the look of delight on Dirk's face, I figured that Daddy had promised him a ride on his tractor-pulled sled. It was an event that had been a highlight to me as I was growing up on the acres of open fields. Now the fun would be shared with another generation of children.

Mother ushered us into the living room. It was obvious that she had been working for weeks. The tree was decorated with ornaments as old as the family name. Underneath was the train, which had waited 12 months in a box just for this occasion. It was an old train, a present to me at one of my earliest Christmases, but to us it was just as good as new. In fact, it was better than new. It had been performing faithfully for years, with nothing to betray its age except its forlorn whistle. The train sped past skiers on snowy peaks and skaters on an octagonal mirror. Every detail of its layout was exquisite.

Heaped around the track were presents. There seemed to

be enough for an army. They came in all sizes, all colors and shapes. It was fun to watch our children sneak glances at the name tags. The fire in the huge brick fireplace crackled its welcome; the cat loved teasing its flames with a daring paw. We could always tell when he had ventured too close. He smelled singed.

Mother excused herself to finish her Christmas baking. We girls had all tried to duplicate her butter cookie recipe, but for some reason our cookies just never came out quite as delicious as hers did. Our mouths watered just anticipating the goodies that would be placed before us in minutes. While we were waiting, we renewed acquaintances: how the children had grown since we last saw one another; and just think, Diane is entering college next fall; how old it makes us feel! As the conversation turned to the baby Lee and I were expecting in the spring, I noticed something that had escaped me in the chaos of the welcome. There on the mantle with all the other Christmas stockings was a tiny one for the expected family member. That's just like Mother, I thought. She doesn't want anybody to be left out.

The festivities that year were as hilarious as I had always remembered them to be. It had become a family tradition to buy silly gifts for one another as stocking stuffers and then to compose appropriate ditties to accompany them. Even new husbands were expected to comply with the tradition. Some of our authors started writing weeks before the anticipated event. Others of us crammed late into the night on Christmas Eve, trying to be more creative than our competition. It usually took us most of Christmas morning to unstuff our stockings and recover from the fun poked at our idiosyncrasies.

That Christmas the gifts were especially cute. Lee, who had recently entered the x-ray business, received a plastic skeleton in his stocking. There was an appropriate warning attached: "This is what happens to all x-ray salesmen who become too involved in their business.'' Daddy, who was sporting a crew cut to ''hide'' his approaching baldness, received some ''stick-em'' for his few short strands. Mother, who was always talking, got a button for her lip. Polly unwrapped a six-inch safety pin to mend the ''disgraceful rip'' in her bathrobe. The laughs lingered throughout the day.

Giving Daddy a nightgown for Christmas had become part of the tradition. He had never liked those modern things with legs that kept him from ''sleeping free.'' So, we always accommodated him, knowing that he would put on his usual modeling show, extolling the virtues of nightgowns over pajamas. This Christmas was no exception. He twirled himself before us with surprising grace, holding his nightgown out wide to show how much room there was.

Nobody seemed to care that by the end of the day the living room was strewn with paper. Each guest had stacked his own pile of boxes in his own selected corner of the room. The turkey was smelling better and better. The cat was sprawled by the hearth, obviously exhausted. The rest of us slouched in our chairs, envying the animal's forthrightness.

The dinner was marvelous. Daddy carved the gobbler like a professional, insisting that his sons-in-law take seconds ''just for good measure.'' I noticed that Lee was holding back on his helping of stuffing in order to make room for Mom's apple pie. Our toddlers sat still longer than usual, waiting for the dates that Grandma had stuffed with fondant. The meal, though, wouldn't be complete without the story of Jesus' birth. Daddy reached to the shelf and took down the same old worn book of the nativity that Mother had shared with me as a child. It contained the most beautifully soft pictures of Jesus' mother that I had ever seen. I watched the grandchildren enjoy them as much as we children had. When bedtime came, they scampered upstairs joyfully. The rest of us talked far into the night, savoring every moment of fellowship.

Daddy had been especially generous with his gifts and

himself that year. In retrospect, I wonder if he knew that it was to be his last farmhouse Christmas. As we left to return to our home in New England, his eyes filled with tears. He was always emotional at departures because he never really knew if he would see us again. This time, though, his eyes seemed to portray a special longing.

Six weeks later he was dead. He had eaten his dinner, risen from the table, walked into the hall, and collapsed. That's how fast it had happened. All of us were anticipating it someday. Yet none of us was prepared when it happened.

In the providence of God the baby I was expecting turned out to be twins. Christmas after Christmas those of us who are left, plus our growing families, tried to carry on the holiday routine. But all of us knew that Christmas would never be the same. The stocking stuffers weren't quite as funny as they used to be. There was no modeling session of the latest in men's nightwear. And we mutilated the turkey.

Over the years I've watched my babies grow from infants to boys to teenagers, each age offering its special compensations. Occasionally I look at them and wonder, Why did God take Daddy without letting him see my twins? He would have loved those little guys with all his heart. And they would have loved him, and the farm, and the sled rides behind the tractor. Now that the twins are teenagers and have joined with their older brother in a trumpet trio, playing before hundreds of church people to the glory of God, that old question resurrects itself: Why?

Every moment of unrest I experience has to be submitted afresh to the God who does all things well. I remember my victory at the funeral. One farmer, who had been especially close to Daddy, came up to me in his grief. He looked at the figure in the casket, then looked at my enlarged tummy, and exclaimed, "He had so much to live for!"

It was a thrill from the Lord to be able to return his tears with a smile and add, "But think what He had to die for!"

Mother, of course, took his death the hardest. She held up admirably throughout the funeral preparations. The grief hit her later, after all the relatives had left. She realized that she would have to sell the farmhouse which had been in the family for generations. It was a tough decision but a necessary one. The home would go, but the memories associated with it would last forever. One day as she was sifting through years of these precious memories, the finality of her aloneness struck her.

In the trunk was her wedding dress, lovingly laid aside 32 years before. Pasted in a scrapbook were honeymoon pictures, portraying bliss that was incongruous with the mood in the attic that afternoon. A yellowed handwritten letter fell out, a token of financial tragedy. Mother remembered too well those early years of heartache when hundreds of livestock died, often in a single night. Then her eye caught a newspaper article, thoughtfully clipped for this moment perhaps. It told how Daddy had made an impressive speech at a town meeting at a time when local tempers were flaring over a land development issue. He had asked for "one minute of time for every generation my ancestors have lived in this town." He had gotten the time and a standing ovation. He was a colorful figure. He made enemies as well as friends. But as Mother relived her life with her husband that afternoon in the attic, she knew that if he were alive today, she would willingly repeat her commitment to him in the defeats as well as in the victories of life.

The gamut of emotions she experienced in such a short time was too much for Mother; she broke down and sobbed. Then she had it out with God. When she rose from her knees she was a new woman, determined to make a fresh start in life. She would use her crisis for personal edification. She would "grow in grace, and in the knowledge of our Lord and Saviour Jesus Christ" (2 Pet. 3:18). From that moment on, she set about doing just that.

She moved from her farmhouse in New Jersey to an apartment in New England near us. She joined a dynamic gospel-preaching church and immediately set out to make friends. She made them—lots of them. Each day she set aside a time for personal devotions in the Scriptures and faithfully kept her appointment with God. She evaluated her Christian life to identify her weakest area—her fear of praying in public. Unreservedly, she gave this weakness to the Lord. Then she watched Him turn it into strength in His way. She discovered that the only way to learn to pray in public is to begin to pray in public. So she prayed aloud with other people listening—hesitantly at first, more assuredly as time went by. To her amazement she discovered that her prayer group was filled with women just as frightened of praying as she was. Together they held each other up before God. And together they were strengthened in their spirits.

Mother wanted her life to count for God in a way that touched other people. So she reached out to those whom she knew were hurting inside as much as she was. She started a fellowship group for widows. Together they lunched, together they laughed, and together they cried. One dear widow said to me recently, "What did we ever do before your mother became part of our congregation?"

Today, 17 years after Daddy's death, Mother is a well-adjusted, independent, God-glorifying woman. Her life is a testimony to God's reconstructive power. When she yielded to Him her negative feelings, He reversed her spiral of depression. When she heeded His injunction to act positively whether she felt like it or not, He gave her victory. It was a victory that has encompassed her emotions as well as her actions. For she is being changed "from glory to glory, as by the Spirit of the Lord" (2 Cor. 3:18). And she is enjoying every moment of it.

23. Active Passivity

Christians are very busy people. We can cram so many worthwhile tasks into one day's schedule that it boggles our minds just to think about them, let alone accomplish them. For example, we women might attend a Bible study in the morning, catch a women's missionary luncheon at noon, visit a friend at the hospital during the afternoon hours, chauffeur our kids to a youth function at dinnertime, and attend a church board meeting until midnight.

Such a schedule breeds danger. It makes us think that because we are busy for God, He must be pleased with us. In our minds, activity becomes equated with spirituality.

Do you know that it is possible to be *too* active for God? To attempt to do His work for Him in the efforts of our own flesh? To claim His promises and then try to fulfill them— through our own manipulations?

We are going to discuss three different types of Christians: some that are too active, others that are too passive, and a third group that have learned the marvelous balance of yielding their lives to God and letting Him move through them.

The biblical patriarch Abraham falls into the first category. In the affair he had with his wife's maid Hagar, he became guilty of what I call "active activity." God had promised the aged patriarch a son. And God had intended to fulfill that promise in His own way in His own time. But Abraham got impatient waiting. So he decided to help God out. Bypassing his barren wife Sarah, he became involved with her handmaid. His adultery accomplished what Abraham desired. A child was born to carry his name. But the child was not the ancestor of the Messiah that God's Word had promised. So Abraham had to recommit his life to the Lord and let God move His own way after all.

The result this time was perfect. These "things are an allegory" (Gal. 4:24), God tells us. In other words, "Don't make the same mistake in your life. What *you* do *for* me is not nearly so magnificent as what *I* will do *through* you if you will let me."

An equally dangerous position in the opposite direction is—for want of a better term—"passive passivity." The person moving within this position has, as the saying goes, "his heart so fixed on heaven that he is no earthly good." He reclines in his easy chair waiting for God to provide. He forgets that God has warned, "If any should not work, neither should he eat" (2 Thess. 3:10). This man may pray for a job "if it be the Lord's will." But he expects it to drop out of heaven. He circulates no resumes, schedules no interviews, initiates no action to secure the right position. He waits confidently, for "God takes care of His own."

This is a preposterous position for the Christian to assume. It is man tempting God with his presumptuous faith. Lee sometimes shares the story of a rather pious fellow who got up to go to work one morning, turned on his bedside lamp and got no light. After determining that it was the lamp and not his electrical supply that was faulty, he started to pray. "God, you can fix my lamp," he said. "You are the Father of lights. You gave the original command for light to enter the universe. Now let it enter my lamp."

Confident that his prayer had been heard and answered, our gentleman arose from his knees, walked to his nightstand, and switched on his lamp a second time. Still no light.

At this point he should have gotten smart, but he didn't. He unplugged his lamp, set it on the kitchen table and prayed again, this time giving God more time. "Lord," he pleaded, "I have to leave for work. I would like to have this lamp fixed by the time I return home tonight. I know you hear and answer prayer. I claim your power in the name of your Son. Confidently I wait."

Now before you explode in utter disbelief, let me assure you that silly petitions like this one are being brought to our Lord regularly. And they are being accompanied by the utmost faith. Furthermore, God could answer them if He wanted to, but I doubt that He ever will. For He has given us practical solutions to the practical problems of life and He expects us to use them. When our gentleman returned home from work that day, his lamp was still sitting on the kitchen table as defective as ever.

Our sincere but misguided Christian needs to be asked some questions. For example, in setting out for work that morning why did you drive your car? Could not God have transported you to your destination without physical means? The book of Acts records that God did such a wonder for Philip. Before you left your home why did you fix breakfast for yourself? Could not God have fed you by ravens? God used such means for Elijah in the wilderness. Why did you bother to get dressed? Could not God have clothed you with skins? God did so with Adam and Eve in the garden. The interrogation could continue to include every aspect of life.

As we learned when we studied the raising of Lazarus, the crux of truth lies not in what God *can* do, it lies in what God *does* do. He warns, "Work out your own salvation with fear and trembling. For it is God which worketh in you both to will and to do of his good pleasure" (Phil. 2:12,13).

When the pioneer missionary William Carey faced his church elders with his plan to take the gospel to India, he was rebuffed with the pronouncement, "Brother Carey, if God is going to save the heathen, He'll do so without your help or mine." I have often wondered what would have happened to the modern missionary movement if Carey had allowed this attitude of passive passivity to stop him.

God's desire for His children lies halfway between active activity and passive passivity. It is a state which Francis Schaeffer aptly calls "active passivity."[4] It involves the balance of actively yielding one's will to God and passively waiting for God to move. It is the type of commitment that Mary made upon learning that she had been chosen by God to become the mother of the Messiah. Like Abraham, she could have "helped" God's promise come to pass by initiating a relationship with Joseph. Or, she could have thrown her hands to heaven in fatalistic resignation, saying, "Whatever will be, will be." She did neither. Instead she took the balanced position of actively yielding her body to God and passively letting Him do with her as He desired. She said, "Behold, the handmaid of the Lord; be it unto me according to thy word" (Luke 1:38).

That's the attitude God expects of Christians, "Be it unto me according to thy word." He expects us to know His Word. He expects us to obey His Word. But He does not expect us to manipulate His Word. Being actively passive leads to victorious Christian living. There is no better time to practice this life-style than in the midst of a life-changing crisis.

24. Stages of Suffering

"I refuse this thing in the name of Jesus! I renounce my suffering and claim release."

Have you ever heard a statement like this one? More personally, have you ever discovered it coming from your own lips? Don't be embarrassed if you have. You are in the company of many precious saints, even of the Lord Jesus Christ Himself. But recognize, even as you are making the statement, that release rarely comes from escaping. More commonly it comes through enduring. In other words, it comes God's way, not yours or mine.

In order to overcome our problems, we need to face reality head-on. If we are in trouble, let's admit it. Ignoring it will not make it go away.

I am reminded of a woman who in her need went for help to a friend who is a Christian. "Please pray for me," she pleaded with urgency. "I'm going through a very deep valley."

"Don't say that!" her counselor warned, looking furtively around. "Even mentioning that there *are* such things as valleys is giving a foothold to Satan."

What kind of counseling is that? If God the Father had made such a statement to Christ when *He* asked for help, we would never have been saved from our sins. I'm glad that instead of denying what He had to go through, Christ met His crisis face to face.

Now, understand that confronting our challenges does not necessarily mean that we have to like what we're going through. The Bible says Christ despised the shame of His crisis, the cross. What confrontation does mean is being honest, allowing our natural emotions to express themselves.

Emotions at the time of crises seem to evolve through several stages. First there is rebellion, then resignation, and finally release to victory. Unfortunately, not all Christians reach the last stage. In fact, some never emerge from the first stage. They let a "root of bitterness" spring up within them; "thereby many be defiled" (Heb. 12:15). Whenever a crisis enters a life, anybody's life, it causes tremendous upheaval. It is almost always regarded as an inconvenient thing which is coming at a very inconvenient time, causing great inconvenience to everyone involved. Naturally, we rebel at the entrance of such an intruder. We should not be ashamed of these negative feelings.

We should, however, guard against our rebellious feelings becoming an end in themselves. God never meant for us to become so bitter in our rebellion that we destroy the lives we touch, including our own. Rather, He wants us to use our rebellion as a stepping stone to resignation and then on to eventual victory. The sinless Son of God rebelled at the crisis of the cross. Alone with His Father in the Garden of Gethsemane, He cried from His soul, "Remove this cup from me." But after the cry of rebellion left his lips, resignation immediately took over. "Nevertheless," He added, "not my will, but thine, be done" (Luke 22:42).

This is the point of total commitment to which we all must come. We must turn our lives over to the Father's control regardless of the personal cost. This resignation of ourselves is not meant to be a fatalistic stoicism reflected in the statement, "Well, there's nothing I can do about the situation, so I just might as well grin and bear it." Nor is it meant to produce a self-righteous martyr's attitude such as "This is my cross to bear. I will cherish every minute of pain." Instead, it is to be a voluntary surrender of our wills to the will of One whose plan is perfect.

"Nevertheless," is the word which Christ chose—not the negative "begrudgingly," or the positive "ecstatically," but the realistic "nevertheless." It is a word which indicates a transition in attitude. It admits to normal rebellion without harboring shame. It resigns itself to surrender without granting entrance to bitterness. Release to victory follows. For Christ it was triumph over death and new life in resurrected power.

Down through the ages many men have suffered, but perhaps none so harshly as Job. Within a very short period of time he went from riches to rags: he lost his belongings, he lost his children, and he lost his health as well. At the beginning of his calamities, he naturally rebelled. "Let the day perish wherein I was born" (Job 3:3), he cried. But he did not remain in his rebellion. He came to the peace of resignation. "Though [God] slay me, yet will I trust in him" (13:15), Job said. That commitment was his doorway to victory.

Later, Job affirmed in triumph, "For I know that my redeemer liveth, and that he shall stand at the latter day upon the earth: and though after my skin worms destroy this body, yet in my flesh shall I see God" (19:25,26). This is a remarkable statement coming from anyone. But it is even more remarkable coming from one of the earliest patriarchs because, in speaking of his Redeemer, Job was looking hundreds of years down the corridor of time. He was anticipating the coming of Christ as his Saviour. In speaking of seeing God in his (Job's) resurrected flesh, he was looking not only past the cross but to the end of time itself, He was seeing himself as a participant in the resurrection of all believers. He was anticipating the coming of Christ as his King.

In New Testament times, the apostle Paul endured similar

tragedies. His will rebelled against the will of God. At one point he cried, "Oh wretched man that I am!" (Rom. 7:24). But like Christ and like Job, his "nevertheless" came; he resigned his will to the Lord's. He said, "Christ shall be magnified in my body, whether it be by life, or by death" (Phil. 1:20). In the providence of God, Christ was indeed magnified in Paul's body, by his life and by his death. With this resolve Paul's release to victory came. As he was about to pass into eternity, he evaluated his life with the following statement: "I have fought a good fight, I have finished my course, I have kept the faith: henceforth there is laid up for me a crown of righteousness, which the Lord, the righteous judge, shall give me at that day" (2 Tim. 4:7,8).

Those last words make me think of a friend who died an agonizing death of leukemia. He hated what was happening to his body, but he never complained about the pain. Nor did he become bitter. When people tried to urge him to pray for healing, he returned their urgings with a smile that indicated he knew the Saviour better than they did. "Not my will but *His* be done," he would say over and over again. And God's will *was* done as angels ushered one of God's most precious saints into His eternal kingdom. Our friend had endured hardness "as a good soldier of Jesus Christ," obeying the orders of his Superior Officer unto the end. Job's victory, Paul's victory, and Christ's victory was his also.

What truth did these men know that the rest of us need to share? I believe the answer to that question lies in Paul's much-quoted statement, "I am crucified with Christ: nevertheless I live; yet not I, but Christ liveth in me: and the life which I now live in the flesh I live by the faith of the Son of God, who loved me, and gave himself for me" (Gal. 2:20). He saw that his life was identified with the life of Christ—all the way.

25. The Upward Spiral

In the third chapter of the book of Colossians, the apostle Paul teaches us what he has learned about identification with Christ. We believers share the power of His resurrection, Paul says. "If ye then be risen with Christ, seek those things which are above" (v. 1). We also share the peace of His death: "For ye are dead, and your life is hid with Christ in God" (v. 3). In the fourth verse we learn that we share the Lord's return: "When Christ, who is our life, shall appear, then shall ye also appear with him in glory."

Understanding this identification should produce self-acceptance. We are risen with Christ! He has lifted us above our failures. He has forgiven us our shortcomings. Now why do we not forgive ourselves? God commands us to do so. He says, "Even as Christ forgave you, so also do ye" (v. 13). Although, in the context of the passage, Christ is talking mainly of our responsibility to others, certainly we must include ourselves as objects of our own forgiveness. Without self-forgiveness, there is no self-acceptance. Without self-acceptance, there is no victory.

We must also accept our crises in life. If, as God says, our lives are "hid with Christ in God," then nothing can touch us without first passing through the Lord. To illustrate this point, I place a coin in my left hand. Then I enclose the coin with my fingers. For good measure, I encircle my left hand with my right. The coin is doubly protected. That's how secure we are in Christ. If, in His providence, God does allow a crisis to pass through His love and into our lives, we can be assured that He intends to use it to make us victorious Christians.

In the upward spiral to victory, acceptance of self and situation is followed by positive action toward both. God details this action very clearly in Colossians 3. In fact, He bombards us with commands: "Seek those things which are above" (v. 1), then, "Set your affection on things above" (v. 2). In these verses we learn that love is a matter of the will. It is not the frothy sentiment that our culture paints it to be. We are told to determine what the objects of our affection will be and then to develop our love for those objects. Feelings should accompany, not precipitate, love.

The next command is, "Mortify . . . your members" (v. 5). In other words, kill those things which tend to hurt your Christian testimony: fornication, uncleanness, inordinate affection . . . They will keep you from experiencing victory. God says, "Put off all these; anger, wrath, malice, blasphemy, filthy communication . . ." (v. 8), then put on the new man. By using the phrases "put off" and "put on" in contrast to each other, God teaches the principle of substituting healthy habits for unhealthy ones.

For example, people who are trying to stop smoking will sometimes chew gum as a substitute for puffing their usual cigarette. Those who seek victory over drinking learn to sip a glass of orange juice instead of their usual martini. Christians desiring control of their tongues pause to insert a comment of praise for the negative remark they are thinking.

Life is a series of habits. Establishing good ones in youth makes life easier to cope with later. Once bad habits have become ingrained in our life-style, they are difficult to change; they are not, however, impossible to change. Victory can come but it must come God's way. The unhealthy habit must first be broken, then it should be replaced with one glorifying to God. Don't forget this principle of substitution. Without it there exists an impossible void.

Another command in this chapter is, "Let the peace of God rule in your hearts" (v. 15). Obedience to this injunction requires active passivity. Once the other conditions of victorious living are met, the peace of God naturally follows. It takes yielding, however, to let it "rule." It should be easy to yield to One who showers His children with blessings. Most of the time, though, we are negligent in taking inventory of just how rich we are. God says, "Be ye thankful" (v. 15). Notice the wording. It does not say, "Feel thankful." It says *"Be* thankful." This carefully chosen imperative suggests an attitude of the mind that the practice of thanksgiving helps to develop.

In my own personal life, I am presently working on establishing a pattern of beginning each day with praise. I start with the Lord Himself and His attributes which bless my soul. I praise Him for His love that endures my stubborn will. I thank Him for His holiness and the goal that it sets for my life. I am conscious that His wisdom is available when I need it. His truth shows the error of my way. His grace accepts me where I am, not where I ought to be. His longsuffering awaits my repentance. His goodness and mercy refresh my soul. Just realizing that all of these attributes are present, meeting my own special needs, makes me fall on my face before Him. I find myself exalting His sovereignty with David's words: "Thine, O Lord, is the greatness, and the power, and the glory, and the victory, and the majesty: for all that is in the heaven and in the earth is thine; thine is the kingdom, O Lord, and thou art exalted as head above all" (1 Chron. 29:11).

Next I count my physical blessings. Beginning with the top of my head, I proceed to the tip of my toes. I express gratitude for eyes that see, ears that hear, a tongue that speaks, and feet that walk. Every time I see someone who is missing even one of these blessings, I thank God all over again for the unmerited favor which He has bestowed upon me.

Then I thank God for my family. I name each individual separately and mention one characteristic of his personality that has particularly enriched my life. I think of my husband's sacrificial love, my oldest son Dirk's great desire to excel, Greg's carefree exuberance, and Jeff's sensitivity to spiritual things. I try to forget the spats, the tensions, and the defeats of the previous day. God's mercies are ''new every morning'' (Lam. 3:23).

I enlarge my circle of praise by including my friends. The diversity of their personalities has flavored my life. While one has stimulated me to seek deeper Christian experience, another has contributed the spontaneity of laughter in situations that offer me no humor whatsoever. Still another has prodded me to keep going when quitting seems to be the only way out. And several have offered good advice when I've needed a diversity of information on which to base a decision.

I also thank God for my church where the gospel is preached with fervor. Then I express gratitude for my country where I am still free to worship as I please. And last I praise God for the world that He will someday return to rule. In order to remember each important item in my prayer, I form a simple diagram in my mind. I am in the center of several concentric circles. Closest to me is God. He is followed in order by my family, my friends, my church, my country, and last by my beautiful world. The diagram looks like figure 8.

I intersperse my praise with Bible reading, during which time God speaks to me. This aspect of my day has become so important to me that if I miss it for one reason or another I feel as if I have missed a meal. God says, ''Let the word of Christ dwell in you richly'' (Col. 3:16). Each day I determine to practice this routine whether I feel like it or not. God does not command me to *feel* thankful. He commands me to *be* thank-

Figure 8

ful. He does not say, "Study the Bible if you want to." He says, "Study the Bible whether you want to or not." Victorious Christian living is for the most part not a matter of emotions. It is the exercise of a disciplined will.

Personal edification is important in enriching our outreach to others. And our outreach to others, in turn, is essential to personal victory. The Bible says, "The Lord turned the captivity of Job, when he prayed for his friends" (Job 42:10). He will turn our captivity also as we take our eyes off our own problems and begin to help our brothers solve theirs.

Another series of imperatives, this time interpersonal ones, lace the third chapter of Colossians. They start negatively, "Lie not one to another" (v. 9). Then come the positive ones: "Put on . . . bowels of mercies, kindness, humbleness of mind, meekness, longsuffering" (v. 12). Interfamily relationships follow: "Wives, submit yourselves unto your own husbands, as it is fit in the Lord. Husbands, love your wives, and be not bitter against them. Children, obey your parents in all things: for this is well pleasing unto the Lord. Fathers, provoke not your children to anger, lest they be discouraged" (vv. 18-21).

All of these statements are commands, not options. They touch every aspect of our lives. God sums them up with an all-encompassing imperative: "Whatsoever ye do, do it heartily, as to the Lord, and not unto men; knowing that of the Lord ye shall receive the reward of the inheritance: for ye serve the Lord Christ" (vv. 23,24). If we are obeying God's instructions in this chapter we are climbing His spiral to victory. Furthermore, as we make this climb of obedience we are learning how to live to His glory. A nobler purpose for human existence cannot be found. For indeed it is God's reason for indwelling us.

26. Identification with Christ

God's indwelling us means that we are identified with Jesus Christ in the same emotions He experienced here on earth. As He rebelled against His crisis, so do we rebel against ours. As He resigned Himself to enduring it, so must we come to the same resignation. And, finally, as He was released to glorious victory, so must we strive for a similar release.

We have learned that victory comes not from feelings but from obedience. There are scriptural principles God expects us to practice; then we too can be on top of our problems. But victory also comes another way. It comes through our willingness to be humbled, even humiliated, if need be, so that God can lift us in exaltation. Such a process was the pattern of Christ's life.

Christ's Earthly Ministry

State of Humiliation	*State of Exaltation*
1. Birth	4. Return
2. Suffering	3. Intercession
3. Death	2. Ascension
4. Burial	1. Resurrection

Figure 9

Before time ever began, Christ was the One who called the universe into existence. The Bible says, "All things were made by him; and without him was not any thing made" (John 1:3). But this Jesus Christ, the Creator, left His glory in heaven, submitted His will to the Father's, and condescended to become one of the smallest particles of His creation: a single cell. Then the one cell divided into many. The many cells became a fetus. The fetus struggled through a birth canal and Christ became *incarnate*, "God-infleshed." After birth He began a childhood of dependency. He who had known no limits of time began moving through a sequence of events. He who had existed everywhere at once became confined to the space of a body. This body experienced need—it hungered, it thirsted, it grew weary and faint. But this was the body that was housing the God of all creation. It was part of the humiliation of Christ.

As Jesus grew in stature, He grew in *suffering* also. Those whom He had created rejected Him as Lord. They brought Him before magistrates in the mockery of a trial. They robed Him as a king, and crowned His head with thorns. They spat in His face, lashed His flesh, and freely blasphemed His deity. Yet He continued to give them breath to do so. Finally they crucified Him, having fashioned a cross from one of the trees He had made. There He hung in agony, His blood, "a river of anguish; His nerves, strands of fire" (Baxter).

Mercifully *death* came. He who had given life to mankind allowed Himself to suffer its grossest indignity: He became "sin for us, who knew no sin; that we might be made the righteousness of God in Him" (2 Cor. 5:21). When His enemies were certain that there was no life left, they permitted His body to be taken from the cross and buried it by placing it in a borrowed tomb. Carefully they guarded the site to make sure that His influence stopped in that cave.

What folly! Death could not hold the Lord. With *resurrection* power He broke its bonds, appearing before His disciples in the very same body which had been crucified three days before. He challenged the doubting Thomas, "Reach hither thy finger, and behold my hands; and reach hither thy hand, and thrust it into my side" (John 20:27). It became evident to all who beheld Him that the corruptible had put on incorruption. Death had been "swallowed up in victory" (1 Cor. 15:54). The resurrection of Christ marked the exciting beginning of a progression of events that would restore Him to His rightful position in glory.

Then one day, while Jesus was standing on the Mount of Olives with His disciples, He was suddenly "taken up; and a cloud received him out of their sight" (Acts 1:9). What a remarkable event! There were no rockets of fire to signal His lift-off, no dials to be checked and rechecked, no oxygen masks to sustain life. There was just the One who said, "I AM life." He *ascended,* and He was returning to His Father.

With His arrival in heaven came great honor. The Father seated Him at His own right hand. Although this elevated position gave Christ no more control of earthly circumstances than He had when He visited our planet (at any moment He could have snapped His fingers and sent His tormentors to hell), it did give Him a different perspective. For now He looked down at earth's problems. The same tensions, strife, and pain that He had experienced were still plaguing the human race. But from heaven it was easier to see the end from the beginning, to observe the good being worked through evil, to marvel at the glory of suffering.

Unless those of us who are struggling with life's crises allow ourselves to be identified with Christ in His ascension, we will not benefit from His perspective. We will continue to wander through bewildering mazes of temptation, finding no real exits to glory. But even in this state of confusion, God is at our side. He promises, "There hath no temptation taken you but such as is common to man: but God is faithful, who will not suffer you to be tempted above that ye are able; but will with the temptation also make a way to escape, that ye may be able to bear it" (1 Cor. 10:13).

In order to help us endure temptation, Christ has establish a ministry of *intercession*. At His Father's right hand He is pleading today—for you, for me, for all who will trust Him to help them. Isn't it thrilling to realize that He knows our every problem? To be able to trust Him with the details, no matter how complicated they may be? To know that if we let Him, He will transport us spiritually to His position in glory where we can view our problems from His perspective?

From His final position of exaltation Jesus Christ will *return* to earth. He will visit again the source of His suffering but this time as King, His sovereignty manifested openly.

Christ's coming victory belongs to any of us who want it. But in order to receive it, we must follow Christ's route! We must also go through those two states: humiliation and exaltation. Humiliation must precede exaltation. Taking that first step down is the hardest. It requires leaving our self-glory with God, confessing our shortcomings in true repentance, and receiving Christ's forgiveness by faith. It means being "born again" or being identified with Christ in His birth. Thus begins our state of humiliation.

Once we have become members of the family of God, it is quite natural to want all the riches that the Father has available and to want them immediately. There is a tendency for new Christians to try to leap from spiritual birth to spiritual resurrection without taking any of the steps in between. We want instant spiritual maturity. It is interesting to note that the apostle Paul expressed a similar yearning, but he knew enough theology to realize that the power of resurrection comes through being identified with Christ's suffering. He longed to "know him, and the power of his resurrection, and the fellowship of his sufferings, being made conformable unto his death; if by any means I might attain unto the resurrection of the dead" (Phil. 3:10,11).

Like Paul, my sufferings in life are my gateway to resurrection power. Before resurrection, however, comes death. Not physical death, in this case, but death to those old patterns of life that are exalting to self and restraining upon God. Remember Paul's words, "Mortify your members." This is a hard command to obey because old patterns sometimes die slowly. But they do die if you replace them with edifying ones. And once they are dead they can be buried forever—along with guilt, pain, and nagging memories.

Jesus Christ came to earth "to bind up the brokenhearted, to proclaim liberty to the captives, and the opening of the prison to them that are bound" (Isa. 61:1). Since God has opened the way, we can emerge from our confining life-styles into His glorious freedom. Bursting from the narrow tomb of self, we can experience His power, power over physical restraints, power over depression—spiritual power, effectual power; power to rise above the crises of our lives, to be seated with Christ in the heavenlies, to view life from God's perspective, to see the purpose of suffering, to be used in intercession for another soul. Victorious power. Christ's power. Wouldn't you like to have that type of power today?

Let me ask you some questions. Have you ever sat at the feet of the King and heard His glorious teachings? Have you ever sunk to His despair then risen to share His victory? Christ is adequate to meet your need. Available to you is strength not only to experience resurrection power but to return to the source of your sufferings, just as Christ returned to His. For some of you that source of suffering is a mate; for others a child, for still others a difficult job situation. Wherever you have to return, however, just remember that you can return victorious. For the King of kings is living within.

Perhaps you are wondering whether victory experienced once lasts forever. In other words, is this identification with Christ's suffering and resurrection a once-for-all-time event? The answer is no. Just as there is no instant growth for a fruit tree, there is no instant spirituality in the Christian life. Fruit comes through the process of growing. There are many ups and downs in learning to become holy. The steps of humiliation and exaltation may have to be walked again and again. No sooner do we receive victory in one area of life than trouble crops up in another area. Another aspect of self may need to die. Then when it's dead we hold another funeral and claim Christ's power of resurrection again.

Occasionally, guilt that we thought we had successfully dealt with years ago resurrects itself with the same old threat we thought we had conquered. It is always a shock to be reminded that evil as well as good possesses a degree of resurrection power. When this happens, we just have to mortify that guilt again. Remember that Christ is more powerful than Satan. Remember too that you may have to die to self in many areas of your life before you receive lasting victory. Becoming like Christ is a continuous process. But victory is there. And it can be yours.

Life consists of both peak and valley experiences. Why should we expect to leap from summit to summit without descending the valleys in between? The peaks are the routes to the valleys. And the valleys are the routes to the peaks. The peaks are the most enjoyable parts of life's journey, to be sure; but they are not the most productive. It is in the valleys that Christian growth occurs. When the showers of God's blessings touch the heights of success and elation, they bring refreshment that will wash into the valley below, just when its soil needs refreshment the most. The farther the waters run downward, the richer they become. Finally they reach the ground that is parched with suffering, preparing it richly for the reception of God's Word. Then, when the seed is sown, a plant establishes itself quickly. Its roots stretch deep. Its fruit forms big and luscious. Only in the valley will such productivity occur, never on the mountain peaks. Peaks are beautiful but stark. The valleys of life are essential to growth.

27. Personal Thoughts

"Lord, this life is not easy. There seem to be more people in the valleys of depression than there are on the mountain peaks of victory. I wish I could solve their problems for them. But only you can do that.

"Father, it is good to know that you control every circumstance of life. As I look back now upon my own rough places in the road, I can see your hand of blessing in every one, especially in our move to Detroit. How I thank you, Lord, that when we were wavering in our trust, your faithfulness abounded anyway. You really *were* working our difficulties to your glory, weren't you? As a family, we still praise you today.

"Thank you especially for my mother. It is settling to know that now, after nearly 17 years of living alone, she wouldn't trade her closer relationship to you for anything in the world. You have dealt magnificently with her. I am eternally grateful.

"I am concerned, though, about the new widow in our congregation. She knows you, Lord, as intimately as my mother does. And she knows you never forsake your own. But there are times, Lord, when it *seems* that you are absent. Oh, please be her portion today. Meet every need that is present.

"I think of our friends whose daughter has run away from home. Lord, these brand new Christians will have to learn quickly what it means to partake of your sufferings. Oh, God, it is hard to suffer. Please give this family victory. And please, Lord, draw their daughter to yourself that she may know that victory too.

"My friend Shirley worries me most. The sieve of divorce is fragmenting her life. Oh, Lord, she needs you desperately; yet she is shunning your every overture. How will you handle her rebellion? What will you do with her crisis?

"I pray for the members of our class in family crises. In my mind I scan their sober faces. Over there is the woman whose husband is battling stomach cancer. She is still being a mighty witness at the hospital. Thank you, Lord, for victory in her valley experience of life.

"To my left is a man going through the termination of his marriage. I recall that after class one night he shared the weight of his failure at what he called 'one of life's biggest challenges.' God, he needs your help.

"To my right is a precious friend whose daughter died at the young age of six. Her eyes reflect the purity of gold—gold refined by fire. The cost of her loss is still there, but so is her glorious triumph. Thank you, Lord, for meeting her need.

"Beside her is a couple whose rebellious son has thrown his religious upbringing to the wind. Together, his parents are agonizing for him to return to the Shepherd's field. Oh God, I pray, give them personal victory whether he comes back to you or not.

"Each face that is familiar to me is reflecting its own special burden. Some of the souls behind the faces are experiencing your power, Lord. Others are still struggling to get it.

"Most of the members of this class are strangers to me. They probably have problems too. I yearn to rub the balm of Gilead into their wounds and watch soothing healing take place. But I can't do your work for you, Lord. I will have to wait for you to move. And that will be in your own way and in your own time, won't it? Give me grace to be patient.''

Sometimes when teaching, we close our last class with a prayer of commitment. It goes like this:

O Christ, I commit myself to you.
I give you my failure, my guilt, my sin.
Give me your victory, I pray.
I will follow in your steps
Wherever you lead me;
I want to bring you glory with my life.

Often the majority of the class joins us in personal surrender to the King of kings and Lord of lords. How exciting! I wonder what would happen if everybody who ever prayed a prayer like that really meant it? How would our world change? Two thousand years ago a handful of committed individuals turned their civilization upside down. They were dedicated disciples of Jesus Christ. They knew the cost of yielding to His lordship, and they were willing to pay it.

I think to myself, *Is the age of pioneer Christianity over? Or is it about to begin again? Is God still making people of fiber tough enough to withstand the pressures of living? Or are we later disciples marshmallow Christians? Soft. Compromising. Sweet but not strong.* I wonder: *What about me? My husband? My children? How would we react if asked to lay down our lives for our faith?*

My thoughts end abruptly. We have just taught our last class on family crises. We receive the comments of our students gratefully, pack up our supplies, and lock the door to our classroom. Hand in hand, we walk down the hall out into the night. The parking lot is full. Friends are discussing the usual trivia of the day. Suddenly a dear brother in Christ approaches, flinging his arm around Lee's shoulder. The two businessmen talk for a while then agree to meet soon for lunch. I know what that means. Another counseling session. Another need for God to meet. The great Counselor is able, I am sure.

As soon as our boys have been dismissed from their respective classes, we start home.

"Look how bright the moon is!" I exclaim. "It's almost as bright as the sun!"

Jeff, our budding astronomer, reminds me, "Mom, the moon doesn't make its own light, you know. It reflects light received from the sun."

I let the remark pass without comment, but it starts me thinking again. *It reflects light received from the sun*. From a distance the moon is an orb of great beauty. But the closer we get to its surface the more the violence of its past becomes evident. Gashes and craters have marred its face, creating scars that will last through its lifetime. But where turmoil once threatened its future, now peace and tranquillity reign.

The moon reflects light received from the sun then transmits it to a world in darkness. Its glow enters hospital windows, reaching souls racked with pain and despair. It illuminates homes and apartments, where tension and strife fill the rooms. It watches while decisions are made—good ones and bad ones. Night after night it shines, constant, faithful, and sure. Its light may be merely a reflection from the sun, I concede. But what a magnificent reflection indeed!

Conclusion

Now that I've come to the end of this study, it's probably time for a little personal evaluation. What has teaching the course on crises done for me? Well, for one thing, it has convinced me more than ever that God is utterly sovereign. He is actively controlling my universe and carefully ordering the events of my life. I know that He wants the very best for me and is creatively working toward that end. This realization brings me much peace.

God has given me new direction. He has snatched me from the folly of self-exaltation and has entrusted me with the privilege of glorifying His holy name. What a responsibility accompanies this privilege! But what reward comes too as God's Spirit provides the enablement!

The more I am getting to know my God, the more I am becoming aware of His involvement in my life. Day after day I sense His presence, nudging me here, restraining me there. Moment by moment I watch Him move, lovingly meeting my every need.

Sometimes I try to box God in, to get Him to minister to me according to my own desires rather than according to His perfect will. But He is patient with me. He reminds me in a diversity of ways that He is infinitely complex in His actions and quite unique in His expressions of love.

In my daily desire to glorify God's name, I often interact with people whose philosophy of life is a constant blasphemy to the Lord I serve. When they are present, I am always on my guard. I find myself torn between wanting to help them find my Saviour's forgiveness and watching lest their destructive influence harm my Christian testimony.

What tension we humans create for each other, I for others and others for me! Add the tension of hectic schedules and trying circumstances, and the pressures of life build within; we all feel them.

Personally, I am learning that if I take no steps toward release and victory, I may plunge to the depths of despair. But God is my present help in trouble. He asks for my burden and promises His peace. When I comply with His request, He is faithful to His Word. He changes my trials into marvelous blessings. And while the glorious transformation is taking place, I find myself growing stronger and stronger in my faith.

In sharing God's bounty with others, I am often asked to explain my own personal formula for victorious Christian living. My answer is always the same. I rely moment by moment on the inner power of God. I have learned that I cannot trust yesterday's blessings to keep me going today. I cannot even rely on my past conversion experience for to-day's spiritual power. If I want present strength to overcome present trials, I must tap the present source of that strength. It is Jesus the Christ, resurrected in power and actively living inside of me.

My growth to spiritual maturity is a matter of self-discipline. It demands Bible study and prayer on a regular, planned basis. Trying always to remember the chief end and purpose of my existence, I talk things over with my Lord every morning.

"How do you want to be glorified today?" I usually ask.

Sometimes the answer comes through the Word of God and requires me to initiate action. "Go ye . . . Pray without ceasing . . . Be reconciled to your brother" are commands I often read. Just as often, however, I read relaxing admonitions, "Be still and know that I am God . . . Think on these things . . . In everything give thanks."

Other times God's answer comes through circumstances. There may be a phone call, a visit, a letter. Then I must be faithful to meet the need that is set before me. What I used to consider interruptions I am learning to regard as divine appointments. For these are God's daily answers to me as to how He wants to be served. Sometimes those answers are marvelously exciting, but more often than not they are horribly routine.

"Get on your hands and knees, Peg, and scrub your kitchen floor," the inner voice may say. When God talks like that to me, I never argue. I just obey. What else is there to do?

Occasionally a crisis will invade my carefully planned day. Then I have to remind myself afresh that how I react to its intrusion will reflect how much control of my life the Holy Spirit really has. I try to hand my resentment directly to the Lord, for I have learned that the longer I entertain oppressive thoughts the more I become accustomed to their presence in my life. Before long I may find myself nursing their growth and encouraging their hold upon my previously victorious attitude. At this point God usually reprimands me, "Cast your burden upon me, Peg, if you want to continue in my victory."

Sometimes I catch on slowly. But the message eventually gets through. My God is faithful to me even when I am not faithful to Him. He thrills to hear my stammering praise, and it does not seem to matter how or when it is uttered. While washing the bathroom tile I may thank Him for my blessings; or while driving the children to school I may evoke the ministry of His angels. Whatever the involvement of the moment happens to be, I know that I can commune with my God and realize His presence in my life. The more I exalt His name, the higher He lifts me from trivia. What an exciting way to live!

I am learning how to trust the Lord for moment-by-moment victories. When I am in pain, He enables me to endure. When I am in health, He encourages me to bask in its blessings. He redeems me from my failures and keeps me from being destroyed by my successes. He assures me that His plan for me is perfect even though I may not understand it at the time I am going through it. As I grow in His grace and in the knowledge of His workings, I want the victorious release that total surrender brings. I want to say with Job of old, "Though God slay me, yet will I trust Him." For He is Lord of my life!

Notes

1. Louis Berkhof, *Summary of Christian Doctrine* (Grand Rapids: Wm. B. Eerdmans Publishing Co., 1939).
2. Elizabeth Elliott, from a taped message delivered at the 1976 Urbana Conference entitled "The Glory of the Will of God."
3. Stuart Briscoe, *Bound for Joy* (Glendale, CA: Regal Books, 1975), p. 19.
4. Francis Schaeffer, *True Spirituality* (Wheaton, IL: Tyndale House Publishers, 1971), p. 58.